Fantasy Baseball Strategy

Advanced Methods for Winning Your League

Henry Lee

SQUEAKY PRESS
P.O. Box 4452
Mountain View, CA 94040-0452
650-967-3200

Copyright © 2004 by Henry Lee
All rights reserved.
No part of this book may be reproduced, stored in a retrieval system, or transmitted by any means, electronic, mechanical, photocopying, recording, or otherwise, without written permission from the author.

For information regarding special discounts for bulk purchases, please contact book@fantasybaseballstrategy.com or visit:
www.fantasybaseballstrategy.com

Manufactured in the United States of America

10 9 8 7 6 5 4 3 2 1

Library of Congress Cataloging-in-Publication data
Lee, Henry.
Fantasy baseball strategy: advanced methods for winning your league / Henry Lee.
p.   cm.
1. Baseball 2. Fantasy baseball (game)

ISBN 0-9748445-0-0

TABLE OF CONTENTS

INTRODUCTION 7

WHY A BOOK ON FANTASY BASEBALL STRATEGY? 8
FANTASY SPORTS, REAL MONEY 8
   Fantasy Magazines and Player Guides 9
   Fantasy Baseball Books 10
STRATEGIES, NOT JUST TACTICS 11
AUTHOR'S PERSPECTIVE 12
HOW TO USE THIS BOOK 13

CHAPTER 1. CHARACTERISTICS OF CHAMPIONS 15

KNOWLEDGE 16
READING THE INDICATORS 17
FLEXIBILITY 18

CHAPTER 2. FUNDAMENTAL THEOREM OF FANTASY SPORTS 21

NO PERFECT INFORMATION 22
FUNDAMENTALS 24
THE ROLE OF LUCK 25
TENACIOUS MANAGEMENT PHENOMENON 26
THE FUNDAMENTAL THEOREM OF FANTASY SPORTS 27
   Case Study 30

CHAPTER 3. COMPETITIVE STRATEGY 35

SUSTAINING COMPETITIVE ADVANTAGE 36
   Cost Leadership 38
   Differentiation 39
BET ON YOURSELF 39
SELF-INTEREST WINS OUT 41
TAKE IT TO THEM! 43
VALUE CREATION 43

CHAPTER 4. VALUATION 45

COMMONLY USED RESOURCES 48
ADJUSTING FOR YOUR LEAGUE 52
   Valuation Methodology 53
   Valuation Example 54
FINDING THE RIGHT MIX 65
   Adding Up the Points 66

ACCOUNTING FOR RESERVES	69
WHERE TO FIND BARGAINS	71
The Draft is Only Half the Battle	*73*
Intelligent Drafting	*74*

CHAPTER 5. SPECIAL CONSIDERATIONS ... 77

THE UNDER APPRECIATED	78
ALLOCATION OF DOLLARS AND SENSE	79
Common Arguments Refuted	*83*
STARTERS VS. RELIEVERS	88
MANAGING FOR STARTING PITCHER INJURIES	92
Pitcher Characteristics	*94*
SPECIALISTS	101
Player Unpredictability	*104*
Case Study	*107*
PLAYERS WITH UNIQUE STATISTICAL CHARACTERISTICS	109

CHAPTER 6. MANAGEMENT STYLE ... 117

BUY AND HOLD	118
ACTIVE MANAGER	119
SEASON MANAGEMENT	120
SUPPORT YOUR STYLE WITH STRATEGY	122

CHAPTER 7. THE DRAFT ... 125

DRAFT TYPE	126
DRAFT DAY DYNAMICS	127
ORGANIZATION	130
DRAFTING FOR DEPTH	131
Depth and Trading Ability	*132*
Allowing for Surprises	*133*
Depth to Support Your Strategy	*134*
Risk Insurance	*136*
HOARDING	137
Price Adjustments	*137*
Piling On	*142*
PREDICTABILITY	145
POSITION SCARCITY	146
Drafting for Scarcity	*149*
SPENDING BASED STRATEGY	152
ROSTER COMPOSITION	154
ADJUSTING MID-DRAFT	156
Anticipate	*156*

Changing Valuations Based on Draft Conditions *157*
Position Depth Knowledge *159*
Price Inflation and Deflation *161*

CHAPTER 8 . FREE AGENTS 167

ANYTHING CAN HAPPEN 168
ROSTER SIZE 170
POSITION PLANNING 172
BEATING THEM TO THE PUNCH 177
   Opportunity Cost *178*
   Player Movement *180*

CHAPTER 9 . TRADING 183

WIN, BUT NOT BY TOO MUCH 184
INCREMENTAL IMPROVEMENT 187
POSITION OVER VALUE 189
UNEVEN PLAYER TRADES 190
GAIN WITHOUT EVER MAKING A TRADE 196
TYPES OF TRADING PARTNERS 197
   The Romantic *197*
   The Cold Caller *200*
   The Negotiator *201*
   The Persuader *203*
   The Apathetic *205*
   The Unpredictable *206*

CHAPTER 10 : KEEPER LEAGUES 209

WHAT IS A KEEPER? 210
LATER MAY NEVER MATERIALIZE 211
OPTION PRICING 215
KEEPER TRADES 218
   Managing Your Keepers *220*
DRAFTING FOR KEEPERS 222

CHAPTER 11 : PUTTING IT ALL TOGETHER 225

STRATEGY CHECKLIST 227
WORKSHEET FOR STRATEGY DEVELOPMENT 232
STRATEGY AIDS AND RESOURCES 237
OTHER ONLINE RESOURCES 237

INDEX 239

TABLES AND FIGURES

TABLE 1: FUNDAMENTAL THEOREM OF FANTASY SPORTS 30
TABLE 2: WHICH TEAM WOULD YOU PICK TO WIN? 40
TABLE 3: HR CATEGORY POINT DISTRIBUTION 56
TABLE 4: POINT DISTRIBUTION RANGES FOR ALL CATEGORIES 57
TABLE 5: PLAYER STATISTICS 58
TABLE 6: CUMULATIVE CATEGORY POINTS 59
TABLE 7: PLAYER BA CONTRIBUTION TO AVERAGE TEAM 61
TABLE 8: PLAYER POINTS 62
TABLE 9: ROSTER TALENT MIX TRADEOFFS 66
TABLE 10: ROSTER CATEGORY STRENGTH 68
TABLE 11: NUMBER OF DL REPORTS PER POSITION 86
TABLE 12: AVERAGE DAYS ON DL 87
TABLE 13: PITCHING STAFF WITH ONE SUPERIOR STARTER 88
TABLE 14: PITCHING STAFF WITH ONE SUPERIOR RELIEVER 89
TABLE 15: PITCHING STAFF WITH THREE SUPERIOR RELIEVERS 90
TABLE 16: STEALS FOR SELECT LEADING BASE STEALERS 105
TABLE 17: GAMES PLAYED FOR LEADING BASE STEALERS 106
TABLE 18: PRICE ADJUSTMENT AFTER HOARDING 139
TABLE 19: PRICE ADJUSTMENT 141
TABLE 20: FUNDAMENTAL THEOREM OF FANTASY SPORTS 144
TABLE 21: ODDS OF DRAFTING AN ACCEPTABLE PLAYER 160
TABLE 22: RELATIVE SPENDING SUMMARY 163
TABLE 23: BOONE/PUJOLS FINAL SEASON STATISTICS 169
TABLE 24: FREE AGENT UPSIDE PROBABILITY 175
TABLE 25: SENSITIVITY ANALYSIS OF PLAYER UPSIDE 176
TABLE 26: OPPORTUNITY COST OF SPECULATING 179
TABLE 27: VALUE EXCHANGE OF UNEVEN TRADE 191
TABLE 28: INITIAL PERCEIVED TRADE VALUE 192
TABLE 29: NET TRADE VALUE 193
TABLE 30: IRREPLACEABLE TALENT 194
TABLE 31: PERCEIVED VALUE FLUCTUATION 214
TABLE 32: STOCK OPTION VALUATION 216
TABLE 33: FANTASY KEEPER VALUATION 217

FIGURE 1: WHEN IN THE DRAFT TO FIND VALUES 72
FIGURE 2: UNIFORM COMPANY FINANCIAL REPORT 79
FIGURE 3: DEPTH PROBABILITY 135
FIGURE 4: KEEPER INFLATION AND DEFLATION 214

Introduction

Why a Book on Fantasy Baseball Strategy?

Books and magazines about fantasy baseball generally do one of two things: Either they tell you the basics of how to set up and play fantasy baseball, or they attempt to give you insight into which players you should draft for your team by assigning values to them. What these publications are missing is that they do not help you win! These books do not provide strategies that will give you a competitive advantage. They are books that provide information, mostly in the form of data. The value of that information is questionable when it comes to actually winning your specific league. It is not that it is inaccurate, just irrelevant.

Certainly, countless hours of baseball research goes into preparing these publications. Many of the leading annuals are fabulous resources for the baseball enthusiast. They can be entertaining and engrossing, but they just are not going to do much to help you win your fantasy league. Valuing players is only a small portion of what you need to do to dominate your league consistently.

Fantasy Sports, Real Money

There is no doubt that fantasy baseball and fantasy sports in general are tremendously popular. Just go to ESPN.com, Sportsline.com, or Yahoo.com and you will find thousands of leagues. In fact, according to CNNMoney[1], over 15 million people participate in

---

[1] Isadore, C., "The Ultimate Fantasy – Profits". Sept. 2, 2003 <http://money.cnn.com/2003/08/29/commentary/column_sportsbiz/sportsbiz/>

fantasy leagues. While football has surpassed baseball in popularity, fantasy baseball is the oldest and arguably the most intense fantasy sport. The Fantasy Sports Trade Association[2] estimates of those 15 million fantasy leaguers, 63% play in fantasy baseball leagues, have an average income of $76,000, and spend an average of $120 per year on fantasy sports. The fantasy sports industry generated $1.8 billion in 2002 and experts expect that number to increase dramatically each year. Fantasy gamers are not only willing to pay to enroll in these leagues, in many, if not most leagues, there is much more money wagered on the outcome of the season. It is typical for a 12-team league to have an "entrance fee" of $100 per team. Leagues usually distribute that $1,200 pot to the winner or top few teams. This is in addition to all the magazines and subscription services fantasy owners pay for each season. With so much at stake, and so much invested, including bragging rights over friends for the rest of the year, fantasy gamers are always looking for an advantage – as they should be.

Fantasy Magazines and Player Guides

It is fantasy tradition in many leagues to go to the bookstore and load up on the new magazines that rank players by their fantasy values. Everyone does it, and most buy several so no one else gets a leg up on them. This is a great business for the publishers of such magazines because every year, gamers need to purchase the latest version with updated statistics and player values. Like an annuity, the money flows out of fantasy

---

[2] Jim Hu., "Sites See Big Season for Fantasy Sports". Aug. 8, 2003 <http://news.com.com/2100-1026-5061351.html>

gamers' pockets and into the magazine publishers'.

The problem with these magazines is that by themselves, they do not help you win because everyone has the same information. Several other members of your league have certainly studied the magazine you have. The bulk of the information in these publications, namely player statistics, is also available on the Internet. Some may claim to have a fabulous proprietary system for projecting future performance, but just about every free source has projections. If you look at enough sources, you will know which players are likely to do well. So will your competition. If everyone has the same information, who gains?

Fantasy Baseball Books

While there are many books on baseball in general, there are actually very few books about winning at fantasy baseball. Several books offer interesting baseball insights by analyzing player statistics, but they only loosely apply to winning your league. Most books about fantasy baseball tell you how to set up a league, the rules, and some basic cookie cutter strategies that can be summed up in convenient acronyms. You can think of these as popcorn strategies. They are light and airy with very little substance. Most people in your league will have heard of such gimmick strategies before. They may have worked for you once or twice in the past, but every league learns quickly. With the Internet, these tricks are fully exposed. Some books advocate standard "Rotisserie" format or some other variation. In many cases, these will guide you towards an affiliated premium subscription or league service so they too have a stake. Someone can tell you the basics of how to play fantasy baseball in about 15 minutes. You do not need a book for that. The most important thing about these books is to know that almost every league you enter in will be different from another league. Advanced league administration software and online services let the league commissioner tweak the rules in multiple ways. Why read about the rules of one league, when your league is different?

Strategies, Not Just Tactics

Strategies are big picture methods for winning your league. Which information source to use and the like are simply tactics or tools. Details matter, but not nearly as much as the strategies you implement. This book will show you how to create a strategy that fits your style, and guide you through the steps you will need to execute that strategy. Flip through the table of contents and you will see that there is much more to winning fantasy baseball than evaluating players.

To win and not simply participate in your league, you have to be more than a spectator. You have to come up with strategies and put them to work. If you have ever questioned the moves of your favorite Major League Baseball team's manager or GM, this is your chance to back up your words. Don't just be the guy yelling down from the cheap seats. If you think you can manage a baseball team better than the next guy, prove it. Win your league!

Execution is the key. Most people have a general strategy going into the draft, but they never think about it again once the season starts. Your strategy should guide your actions before the draft, during, and after. It should guide your actions when you are attempting to make a trade or trying to pick up a free agent. If you are not aware of how any move you make fits in with your strategy, you are just winging it – and you will be lucky to finish well in your league.

This book will help fantasy baseball owners of all levels. Beginning fantasy team owners will obtain a level of insight that many experienced fantasy-goers have never even considered. Experienced fantasy team owners will be able to apply the knowledge they have gained about themselves and their leagues to a customized strategy that will benefit them throughout the season.

Author's Perspective

What makes me an expert at fantasy baseball? I know how to win. That is the bottom line. While I have participated in many types of leagues, I have been in the same league for the past 10 years and have won it five times. With 11 other smart, successful baseball fanatics, my winning is not a coincidence. I must be doing something right. There are definitely people who know baseball better than I do. Very few know how to win at fantasy baseball better than I do.

My approach to devising strategies may come from my career background. No, I am not a professional fantasy baseball gamer. If you know of anyone hiring for such a job, let me know. I used to be in the business of teaching communication and management skills. Later, I went on to trade stocks for a living. Maybe having made over 30,000 stock trades gives me a better sense of fantasy baseball trades than others have. I also happen have an MBA so I might tend to look at strategy from a business perspective. I am not sure if my background makes me any more or less qualified to write a book about fantasy baseball strategy, but knowing it might give you a sense of where I am coming from as you read.

It would be impossible to write a book from the exact perspective of every fantasy league owner. There are simply too many different kinds of leagues. The approach I take is to give specific examples to general situations that occur in fantasy baseball. You have chosen to read this book so you probably understand the importance of strategy. I assume you are smarter than the average fantasy owner is. I have faith that you will be able to draw the right conclusions of how it applies to your league and its rules.

When I write about the draft, I use it as a generic term for an auction. Straight and snake drafts may not have to deal with bidding tactics, but many of the same strategic objectives still apply. Consider draft and auction as interchangeable words for the rest of this book. Also, assume scoring to be on accumulated player statistics. I also use quite a few examples of a league I have been in for the past 10 years. It happens to be a Mixed[3] 5x5 Fantasy[4] league, but the concepts the examples illustrate should apply to all kinds of leagues. Shifting back and forth between league types would be confusing and difficult to read. As I stated earlier, I believe you will be able to see how the examples apply to your league.

How to Use this Book

You can use this book as a reference guide to use at the draft and throughout the season. I recommend

---

[3] Mixed refers to a league including players from the AL and NL
[4] Standard 5x5 Fantasy categories are AVG, RBI, HR, SB, R and W, SV, WHIP, ERA, SO. Rotisserie 4x4 does not count R or SO.

that you read it through once from start to finish. At the end of each chapter are a few questions to stimulate your strategic thinking. Jot down your initial thoughts. It will help solidify your understanding of how the concepts apply to your league and become a valuable reference later on. Then, refer back to the various chapters as you go through the process of formulating your strategies. At the end of the book is a worksheet to fill out your strategies. There is also a checklist to make sure you have not forgotten anything important. Bring your book to the draft. At the very least, it will intimidate your opponents to no end. During the draft, refer back to your strategy worksheet to make sure you are sticking to your strategy. Also, run through the checklist at lulls in your draft to keep you focused. If your draft performance fits into your strategy and can pass the checklist, you will surely be a dominant force in your league every single season.

Which people in your league do you think have a comprehensive strategy going into the draft?

How do they compare competitively with the people who have no apparent strategy?

Chapter 1. Characteristics of Champions

16   *Characteristics of Champions*

So what qualities make for a successful fantasy league owner? People who tend to be good at fantasy leagues seem to have a few common traits. If you do not think you strongly exhibit these characteristics in your daily life, you can still be a very good fantasy league owner simply by becoming aware of them.

Knowledge

Knowledge is the base. It would be difficult to do well in your league if you are not knowledgeable about baseball in general and the nuances of your league in particular. There simply is no substitute for knowledge. Your league will probably turn over a couple of owners each year. New owners will generally be at a disadvantage because they are unfamiliar with the rules of your league, or more likely, because they are unfamiliar with the tendencies of the other owners in the league. If it turns out that the new owners just are not big enough fans of baseball to keep up with all the information it takes to compete in your league, they will soon drop out.

While owners tend to evaluate the expected contributions of individual players similarly, you might be able to gain an advantage when it comes to the valuation of players relative to your league's rules. Most owners are aware of what the annual magazines player projections are, but they also tend to rely on them too much. One obvious mistake fantasy baseball owners make is basing their player values on the projections of magazines catering to leagues that score using different categories. Some magazines rank

Fantasy Baseball Strategy

players on the traditional rotisserie 4x4 scoring[5] while others rank them using Fantasy 5x5. The least you can do is pick up a magazine that most closely resembles your league rules and scoring. You may also find that your league rules tend to weigh certain statistical categories more heavily than others do. Perhaps, your league tends to favor pitchers more than hitters so the dollar amounts of pitchers in those magazines will tend to be low. No magazine will evaluate players exactly how the members of your league will. Note the differences and adjust your rankings accordingly.

Reading the Indicators

Good fantasy owners tend to be observant people. They monitor their opponents' likes and dislikes. They notice if teams tend to go after unknown players on a hot streak, or prefer players with a consistent record of accomplishment. In short, they are able to garner and process more information from disparate sources than others.

Indicator reading occurs at the draft when all the owners are sitting around the same room. It also occurs during the season when most owners have gone their separate ways. Rumors and minor team transactions may indicate important events to come. It takes anticipation and intuition to be in the hunt for the next hot free agent or to trade away the closer who will eventually become a middle reliever on another team.

Good fantasy owners keep track of what their opponents try to do.

---

[5] Rotisserie 4x4 categories are AVG, RBI, HR, SB and W, SV, WHIP, ERA

Characteristics of Champions

Good fantasy owners keep track of what their opponents try to do. One excellent technique for getting a better feel for how the other owners think is to write down which owners made the next to last bid on the players you ended up with at the draft. That should indicate to you which owners will likely be the most receptive to your trade offers. If they wanted your players at the draft, they will probably want them later. Good owners also take note of which players other owners attempted to pick up as free agents. Even if they do not end up with them, knowing which players to offer them in trades, or simply the types of players they prefer is valuable information.

Flexibility

If there is one thing that you should keep in mind when preparing your strategy, it is that something unexpected could occur. Your strategy should not be so rigid that if things do not happen as you had anticipated, you will not know what to do. If suddenly during the draft, you realize that some of the tactics you were planning to use will be ineffective, you must be willing to change. Suppose part of your strategy was to draft the top catcher, the top shortstop, and the top second baseman as the core of your team. Then, you realize that the demand for these premium players is much greater than you had anticipated. Should you bid 20% more than you had expected for each one, knowing that it will hinder your ability to draft other

> *By exercising your imagination before the draft, you can anticipate how your primary strategies may go awry.*

Fantasy Baseball Strategy   19

players you thought would be available at bargain prices? That of course depends on how crucial those players are to your strategy. It would be smart though to be flexible enough to change directions should the price become too high. There should always be a point in your mind where the costs outweigh the benefits.

Flexibility comes from stretching beforehand. By exercising your imagination before the draft, you can anticipate how your primary strategies may go awry. You want to think ahead and envision how the other owners in your league might react to your methods. Perhaps the other owners will do something unorthodox so early in the draft that you will not even have time to initiate your strategies.

If you can exhibit these characteristics, you should be able to implement strategies for winning your league.

By anticipating what could go wrong, you will be prepared when unexpected events inevitably do happen. In the draft, while deciding to pull off a trade, or picking up a free agent, those who did not anticipate well will falter. Owners that have not prepared to be more flexible by stretching their imaginations will snap under pressure. You will be able to bend strategies to conform to any situation.

Do your best to be knowledgeable about what is going on in baseball and how your league works. Read the indicators that other owners give off and anticipate their moves before they occur. Stay flexible, by accounting for the unexpected in your strategies. Plan for these occurrences and you will be able to react to them with greater effectiveness. If you can exhibit these characteristics in your league, you should be able to implement strategies for winning your league.

Who are the strongest competitors in your league?

_____
_____
_____
_____
_____

What do you think makes them so strong?

_____
_____
_____
_____

What can you do to emulate their strengths?

_____
_____
_____
_____

Chapter 2. Fundamental Theorem of Fantasy Sports

No Perfect Information

Have you ever picked up a magazine of the world's richest individuals and noticed that a high percentage of them amassed their wealth through real estate? There must be something to that. A real estate developer friend of mine said it was because there are a handful of individuals that have much better information than 99.9999% of the population. There are many globally known real estate tycoons, but most of them concentrate their investments regionally as Donald Trump does in New York and New Jersey. This is because they are masters of their domain. Intimately knowing the territory they play in has great advantages. They know the nuances of doing a deal there, the best locations, the hands to shake, the palms to grease, and how to push through local commissions better than anyone else does.

Knowing that I used to trade stocks for a living, my friend explained to me that there is, in effect, what economists call "perfect information" in the stock market. However, there is not in real estate. There is a common theory about the stock market that when you hear a tip about a particular stock, many others have already heard that tip and have acted upon it. They have already traded the stock and it has gone up or down accordingly. There are thousands of transactions each day on a given stock so the market adjusts very quickly. Thus, the market adjusts as if it were perfectly informed. In real estate, a piece of property may not sell for years so it is difficult

As a fantasy baseball owner, there are lessons you can learn from real estate tycoons.

Fantasy Baseball Strategy 23

for an outsider to know what a fair price for that property is. There is so much time between real estate transactions that quite a bit of value may not be accounted for since the last time a price was established. Those who know the territory well have a better feel for the actual value. Special knowledge of hidden value in the stock market is called "insider trading" and is illegal. Insider trading in real estate is called good deal making.

Your job as a fantasy baseball owner should be to obtain better information than your opponents are able to obtain. There is no perfect information in fantasy baseball. If you get a tip about a minor league call-up, not everyone in your league will know about it. You are free to take advantage of any information you possess. You are also free to gather information about your league and those who participate in it. Synthesize all that information as a real estate mogul would to help you acquire players at bargain prices, allow them to gain value, and sell them off for greater value.

There is no perfect information in fantasy baseball. Your job should be to obtain better information than your opponents are able to obtain.

As a fantasy baseball owner, there are lessons you can learn from real estate tycoons:

- Know your league (territory) better than anyone else does.
- Strive to obtain better information than your opponents have.
- "Insider trading" is legal. Benefit from acting on information you and few others possess.

- Choose players strategically so you can build them up and sell them off.
- Obtain insights about your players (investments), but also your competition.
- Make sense of information so that it becomes an advantage to you.

Fundamentals

Know more than your competition. Knowledge translates into value. Every time you acquire a player for less than he is worth, you win and your competition loses. Studying the players is the first thing you need to do, but knowledge is more than what you can read in a magazine. There will always be trends that emerge in your league. All trends are temporary. You might observe that the members of your league tend to overbid on hyped rookies, and underbid second year players who disappointed as rookies. Maybe two owners in your league from New York tend to overbid on Yankee players, and underbid on Red Sox players. In poker, you look for another player's "tell." You observe patterns that emerge that will give you information on what your opponent will do. These trends can be used to your advantage until everyone else recognizes them as well. The key is to identify

The key is to identify the trends before your competition does. When enough people are aware of the trend, the value of that knowledge goes away.

the trends **before** your competition does. When enough people are aware of the trend, the value of that knowledge goes away. This is the main reason why widely followed stat services provide very little marginal value to your chances of winning. It is good to know because everyone else knows it, but it does not provide that edge.

The Role of Luck

Jon Gruden, head football coach of the Tampa Bay Buccaneers, sleeps only four hours a night. During the season, he dedicates all his waking hours to thinking about football. Does that mean he is the best coach? No. Does that mean he is more prepared than everyone else is? No. It means he is prepared and that the likelihood that another coach's game day strategy will surprise his team is slim. If his team's strategy is wrong, it will be because it was his decision to prepare his team that way, not because of something the opposition did. He does his best to prepare his team by anticipating what his opponents may do. By doing that, he can coach his team during games closer to how he coached it in practice. The fewer surprises, the more he minimizes the mistakes and maximizes the gains.

Baseball is a great game, because on any given day, a mediocre pitcher can completely dominate the lineup of a top team. A hitter can go 4 for 4 with a HR and 3 RBI at any time. You simply cannot predict what exactly will happen. What you can do is gauge the trends and position your team to take advantage of what will likely happen. You might properly prepare yourself having defined your strategy, evaluated every player, read every news article, and negotiated trades skillfully, but you still will not win without a little luck.

Every year, players come out of nowhere to have career years. Usually dependable stars can suffer debilitating injuries or inexplicably become mediocre.

The Fundamental Theorem

Some years you will get your fair share of luck. Those are the years that if you are prepared, you will have a great chance of winning. If you do a good job of preparing and doing all of the things winning fantasy baseball teams do, you should consistently end up in the top half to top third of your league. The years when luck falls on your side, you will be in position to win.

Luck plays a large role in every fantasy league. For the most part, injuries are hard to predict and can happen at any time. Marginal players can have breakout years without any prior indication. Luck probably accounts for a variance of 25% in expected performance each year. That is an estimate since it would be difficult to measure and there are few studies circulating about fantasy baseball luck. If you can accept that figure, the rest is up to you. You need to put yourself into position so you have a chance to win. You can have some phenomenal surprises, but if you draft poorly and do not trade well, you will not win. Sometimes luck will be on your side, sometimes it will not. When it is on your side, you will always have a great chance of winning by doing the other things well.

Luck probably accounts for a variance of 25% in expected performance each year. The rest is up to you.

Tenacious Management Phenomenon

A phenomenon occurs at the tail end of each season in many leagues. It usually becomes clear that some teams are going for the win and others are giving up. This phenomenon is most common in keeper leagues where owners consciously trade away top

Fantasy Baseball Strategy

players for players that represent future values. Those trading for this year are going for it and those trading for the future are giving up. A team with a solid strategy, earnestly trying to win - no matter where they are in the standings or what kind of bad luck they have experienced – will finish in the top half of the league with virtual certainty. All you can do is place your team in position to win. More often than not, you will be in the mix at the end. Chapter 7: The Draft will discuss strategies to take advantage of the Phenomenon.

> *Any team with a solid strategy, earnestly trying to win will finish in the top half of the league with virtual certainty.*

The Fundamental Theorem of Fantasy Sports

Fantasy baseball is a game of limited information. Much like a game of poker, you cannot possibly know exactly how the cards will eventually fall. What you can do is play the odds, make your big bets when the odds are in your favor, and play your opponents. At the highest level of poker, every player knows the odds of every hand. What separates the champions from the rest is their ability to read other players and make them react (or overreact) to their moves. The same is true of fantasy baseball. Just about every team owner has the ability to place reasonable values on individual players. What makes them champions is their ability to read the signals that others miss, and at the same time, influence how competing owners manage their teams. Part of influencing the competition is bluffing or making them think you are going to do one thing, and then doing another.

One excellent way to look at approaching your fantasy league is through the viewpoint of another game. The Fundamental Theorem of Poker as described by David Sklansky best summarizes it.

The Fundamental Theorem of Poker[6]

"Every time you play a hand differently from the way you would have played it if you could see all your opponent's cards, they gain; and every time you play your hand the same way you would have played it if you could see all their cards, they lose. Conversely, every time opponents play their hands differently from the way they would have if they could see all your cards, you gain; and every time they play their hands the same way they would have played if they could see all your cards, you lose."

In other words, do your best not to let your opponents know the cards you are holding. At the same time, try to figure out what they are holding. If you knew an opponent had a pair of queens and you only had a pair of threes, it is clear that your best move would be to fold and cut your losses. Your decision would be easy. If for some reason, your opponent thought you had two aces, he might fold his hand. Therefore, you can gain by getting a read on your opponent's hand, and you can gain by not letting your opponent get a read on yours.

Make your decisions easy and straightforward and your opponent's decisions difficult and unclear.

---

[6] Sklansky, D. *The Theory of Poker*. Henderson, NV: Two Plus Two Publishing, 1999. p. 16

In fantasy baseball and fantasy sports in general, you want to make your decisions as easy and straightforward as possible and make your opponent's decisions difficult and unclear as possible. You can make your decisions easier by understanding your opponents, their teams' needs, and their strategies. Make your opponents decisions difficult by making your strategies unpredictable and hard to figure out. Translating Sklansky's poker version into fantasy sports:

Fundamental Theorem of Fantasy Sports

"Every time you manage your team differently from the way you would have managed it if you knew what your opponents' strategy were, they gain; and every time you manage your team the way you would have managed it if you knew what your opponents' strategy were, they lose. Conversely, every time opponents manage their teams differently from the way they would have managed them if they knew your strategy, you gain; and every time they manage their teams the same way they would have managed them if they knew your strategy, you lose."

Of course, it is unlikely that you will know exactly what your opponent's strategy will be. Nor is it likely that he will know yours. Obviously, you want to keep your strategy to yourself. It does not mean that you should be deceitful, but broadcasting your strategy will put you at a disadvantage. The more your opponents know about your strategy, the more likely they are to carry out their plans unimpeded. The point is to make your opponents do something they do not want to do or something they would not have done had they better anticipated your strategy. You should anticipate what they are likely to do, and plan what you want to happen. Either the league will react to you, or you will react to the league.

Table 1: Fundamental Theorem of Fantasy Sports

If all strategies were known		You	
		Manage the Same	**Manage Differently**
Opponents	**Manage the Same**	You Benefit + Opponents Benefit = **No Clear Advantage**	You Lose + Opponents Benefit = **Advantage Opponents**
	Manage Differently	You Benefit + Opponents Lose = **Advantage You**	You Lose + Opponents Lose = **No Clear Advantage**

Just like in poker, the outcome in fantasy baseball is not always certain. There are no guarantees that if you play everything the way you wanted to play it, you will win. A good player will play his game, but on any given hand, if the cards do not fall correctly, he could lose to an inferior player. What a good player does is minimize his bets to lose less when the odds are against him, and maximize his bets to win more when the odds are in his favor.

Case Study

One of the owners in your league says to you that he recently heard of a strategy where you select top pitchers and leadoff type hitters at the draft. It is an old

Fantasy Baseball Strategy 31

draft strategy, but it sounded new to him. The theory here is to win all the pitching categories and dominate Steals, BA, and Runs. You do not think much of it because he likes to throw out all sorts of things to get a reaction out of you. Just in case though, you do a little scenario planning in your pre-draft preparation. Your contingency plan is to get the second 35+ steal player that comes up for bid if that owner drafts the first one. If his first two players selected are either speed players or top pitchers, you will make sure to get one of each as well. You want to get your players before the rest of the league catches on. After that, you will continue with your primary strategy that, in part, consists of obtaining top middle infielders.

On draft day, your opponent does indeed draft Juan Pierre and Jason Schmidt as his first two players. Your first two players are Alfonso Soriano and Javier Vasquez. You are happy because you have countered his strategy by getting a top steal threat and a top pitcher. You have also filled one of your middle infield positions with a top player. Your opponent goes on to select Carl Crawford, Scott Podsednik, and Ichiro Suzuki. His team so far looks like:

HITTER	R	HR	RBI	SB	AVG
J. Pierre	100	1	41	65	0.305
C. Crawford	80	5	54	55	0.281
S. Podsednik	100	9	58	43	0.314
I. Suzuki	111	13	62	34	0.312

Pitcher	W	SV	ERA	SO	WHIP
J. Schmidt	17	0	2.34	208	0.95

The two players you have drafted look like this:

The Fundamental Theorem

Hitter	R	HR	RBI	SB	AVG
A. Soriano	114	38	91	35	0.290

Pitcher	W	SV	ERA	SO	WHIP
J. Vazquez	13	0	3.24	241	1.11

At this point in the draft, you think your team is well positioned. Clearly, you will not win SB, but you have the inside track for second place in that category without having to give up HR and RBI. You also have an excellent pitcher. The other owners in the league are left with only the unreliable Alex Sanchez and Dave Roberts as the only 35+ steal threats remaining besides the five-category Carlos Beltran who will surely go for a premium price. All three of these players end up going for at least $5 more than originally projected because of the intense competition for Steals.

Competitively, you rank your team as the leader to this point. It is still mid-draft, the first day of your league and you already think you have the best team in your league. Having some insight into your opponent's strategy – albeit through happenstance – you were ready for his moves and were able to maintain your primary strategy. Your opponent loses to you because his team is now at a disadvantage to yours overall. You will surely dominate his team in the power categories while his only bests yours by one place in the standings in SB. He does however, gain on the rest of the league because they were not able to draft speed and will probably be forced to trade with him if they want to compete.

According to the Fundamental Theorem of Fantasy Sports, you benefit because you managed as if you knew your opponent's strategy, but the rest of the league loses because they bid more than they had expected to bid for speed players, or they did not get one at all. In a 12-team league, you gained advantage over 10 teams because you managed the same and they managed differently than they would have if they knew what the speed-monger was going to do. According to the Theorem, there is no clear advantage gained between you and the speedy team, but because of his strategy, you think your more balanced team has an edge. By applying the Fundamental Theorem of Fantasy Sports to your decision making process throughout the season, you can continue to gain advantages over the other teams in your league.

By applying the Fundamental Theorem of Fantasy Sports to your decision making process throughout the season, you can continue to gain advantages over the other teams in your league.

What is your source of insider information?
_____
_____
_____
_____
_____

The Fundamental Theorem

What trends have you noticed in your league?

How does the Tenacious Management Phenomenon influence your strategies?

How will the Fundamental Theorem of Fantasy Sports help you to win?

Chapter 3. Competitive Strategy

Any move you make directly affects your competition. You can devise all sorts of strategies that may help you put together a solid team, but it is important to know that you have the ability to alter your league's competitive environment. Looking at how successful businesses create competitive advantage can be a guide you can use for your team. Additionally, three competitive strategy elements will help you devise your strategy. First, self-interest wins out. You may agree with this statement on many levels, but in terms of fantasy sports, it simply means that owners will ultimately do what is good for their own team before serving the needs of the collective group. Second, a strategy that forces others to react to it will put you in a position of strength and your opponents in a position of weakness. Third, the draft, free agent acquisitions, or trading are not just places to find value. You can strategically create value for your team by your own actions. If you wait for value to come to you, you must compete against everyone else for it. If you create the value yourself, others will compete amongst themselves to give you the most value. This may sound unbelievable, but it absolutely works.

Sustaining Competitive Advantage

There is a great deal of research done on the subject of competitive strategy. In the business world, probably the most followed authority on the subject is Michael Porter. Porter literally wrote the book, Competitive Advantage[7]. In short, he points out that competitive advantage essentially boils down to cost leadership and differentiation. Think about how this

---

[7] Porter, M. Competitive Advantage. New York: Free Press, 1985

applies to fantasy baseball. If it works for GE, Ikea, Vanguard, The Gap, and other successful businesses, these ideas might give you an edge in your league.

According to Porter, businesses that are able to sustain competitive advantage have several things in common. In terms of fantasy baseball, teams that sustain competitive advantage have these attributes:

Unique competitive position within the league

Something should set your team apart from the other teams in your league. You might have more knowledge, better relationships with the other owners, or an advantage you created during the draft.

Activities are tailored to strategy

When you draft, trade, pick up a free agent, or change your roster, every move should support your strategy. The results of all your moves should add up to more than the sum of the parts.

Clear trade-offs & choices vis-à-vis competitors

Your strategy should provide you an operational guideline for your actions throughout the year. It should be clear to you what your move should be in any given situation. When you are deciding whether to make a trade or not, if it furthers your strategy, do it. If it does not, do not make the trade. It should be clear and simple.

Competitive advantage arises across activities

The season does not end the day of the draft. You do not gain advantage simply by what you do during the

38 *Competitive Strategy*

draft. Every move you make should make your team incrementally better.

Operational effectiveness is a given

You need to operate your team with thought and attention all season. Things like forgetting to change your lineup or not submitting a free agency pick will hurt your team. You have to execute your strategy the way you envisioned it for it to work.

When you put together a strategy for your fantasy baseball league, refer back to this list. You should strive for these attributes. If you can accomplish each point, your team will be in a position to win.

Cost Leadership

Until this book, few baseball authors have written about differentiating your team from the competition. In essence, resources that help you value players – magazines, projections, etc. – are actively advocating the cost leadership strategy. The basic strategy is to obtain as much talent as you can, at the lowest possible cost. If your valuation method is better than your competition's, you will have a competitive advantage. This is a legitimate strategy. Fantasy baseball owners have been using it since the game's inception. Do you see where the problem lies? If you think of your fantasy team as a business, it does not make sense to try to beat the competition by cutting costs if that is what everyone else is doing. Do you have what it takes to cut costs better than 11 other teams? You do not want to compete against Wal-Mart on cost. Are you the Wal-Mart of your league? There could be an actuary or a statistician in your league with a much

Fantasy Baseball Strategy

better sense of the numbers. Thankfully, there is much more to fantasy baseball than just crunching numbers.

Differentiation

Since you know that just about every other team in your league is going go with the cost cutting strategy as they always have, you have a choice. You can follow suit and hope that somehow, your valuation method is the best and that you will be able to draft players for significantly less than they are worth. An alternative is to differentiate your team from the rest and try something else. You can devise a strategy that focuses on trading. You might tailor your team around free agent acquisitions, or take advantage of your league's "keeper" rules. This book will show you how you can create and sustain competitive advantage by utilizing strategies that will set your team apart from the rest.

Create and sustain competitive advantage by utilizing strategies that will set your team apart from the rest.

Bet on Yourself

Let me pose a hypothetical scenario. There are 12 teams in your league. Of those 12 teams, 11 will employ a cost cutting strategy by looking for bargains. One team however, decides to implement a completely different but well thought out and comprehensive strategy. You have to bet on one team. Which one would you bet on to win?

Table 2: Which team would you pick to win?

TEAM	STRATEGY
1	Look for bargains as they come up at the draft
2	Look for bargains as they come up at the draft
3	Look for bargains as they come up at the draft
4	Look for bargains as they come up at the draft
5	Look for bargains as they come up at the draft
6	Look for bargains as they come up at the draft
7	Look for bargains as they come up at the draft
8	Look for bargains as they come up at the draft
9	Look for bargains as they come up at the draft
10	Look for bargains as they come up at the draft
11	Look for bargains as they come up at the draft
12	Conserve money at draft until round seven when performance per dollar value increases dramatically. Monopolize strikeout-type starting pitchers at the draft to create trading imbalance in the league. Teams that need pitching - everyone in contention - will have to trade with you. Become league power broker. Maintain bench flexibility on team so can speculate on free agents without dropping valuable players. Acquire young phenoms early in the season to trade as "keepers" when others fall out of contention.

That was completely unfair, but it does make a point doesn't it? There was no way to distinguish between the other teams in the league. It does not take a genius to pick the team that will have the best chance of winning here. As ridiculous as this scenario seems, does it not depict most leagues fairly well? It certainly does. Most owners study their magazines, put a checkmark next to the players they think have potential, and adjust at the draft. There are no guarantees, but the odds are in one team's favor. You can be that owner. Devise a

Fantasy Baseball Strategy

comprehensive strategy to differentiate yourself from the rest of the league.

Self-Interest Wins Out

Your competition cannot easily counter a solid strategy. The other owners may sniff out your basic strategy – in some cases, it will be blatantly obvious what you are trying to do – but in most cases, they will not be able to prevent you from executing it without hurting their own prospects. If there is one thing you can count on, it is that your opponents will try to do what is best for their teams. They may try to intimidate you by threatening not to trade with you, but take that as an indication that you have put them on the defensive.

A specific example can help illustrate this point. Suppose your strategy is to draft the very best shortstops available. You realize that you may not be able to play them all, so eventually, you will have to trade some of them. This is a strategy I call hoarding (Discussed in Chapter 7) and opponents quickly detect it. Teams notice this strategy as soon as you make your second move, but by then it is too late. For example, having secured Alex Rodriguez as your starting shortstop, you then draft Nomar Garciaparra as your backup. The typical reaction is for several owners to signal the alarm bells warning the others not to trade with you during the season. Your league may very well have rules that prevent such collusion against a single owner, but practically speaking, you should not be worried about finding a trading partner. There will always be demand for an ARod or a Nomar. Most teams would be lucky to have such a productive player as a designated hitter (DH).

Competitive Strategy

In any given season, there may be four premier shortstops, a couple of others that most owners would be happy to have on their teams, and the rest are all serious liabilities in a few categories. In general, with such limited depth at a position, there is little player movement during the season. Those with a premier shortstop are unwilling to trade, and those without cannot pry one loose without giving up an unfair amount of talent in return. In this case, you happen to have two of the top four shortstops in the game. Two teams have one each. In a 12-team league, the remaining nine owners are each left with a barely serviceable shortstop. They may not like the thought of trading with you after your draft day stunt, but faced with the prospect of having to go the rest of the season with a Cesar Izturis at short, they will gladly talk trade individually.

The typical reaction is for several owners to signal the alarm bells warning the others not to trade with you during the season.

Collectively, the other owners will tell each other to hold the line and not trade for your shortstops during the season. Individually, they will try to be your exclusive trading partner. They know that if you trade away your extra shortstop to another one of their competitors, the status quo will hold true once again and there will likely be no more movement at short for the rest of the year. No, not Cesar Izturis!

You can count on the fact that self-interest will win out. If an owner is stubborn enough not to even try to get one of your shortstops, he is probably not going to be a serious contender for the league title in the end.

Fantasy Baseball Strategy

Understand the perspectives of your opponents and you will know exactly how they will react to your moves. According to the Fundamental Theorem, you gain. When you know how your opponents will react, you can devise strategies to manipulate their actions to your benefit.

Take It to Them!

Hoarding shortstops is simply one example of how your strategy affects more than just the draft; it also influences the trading action during the season. This illustrates the primary principle of a good strategy. Make your opposition react to your moves. Most of your opponents will not have as comprehensive a strategy as you will. A few will have an idea of which key players they would like to draft if they are available. *Any owner using an "if available" strategy will be vulnerable to the owner who actively makes those key players unavailable.* Any owner using an "if available" strategy will be vulnerable to the owner who actively makes those key players unavailable. Assuming a 12-team league, would you rather be the one owner with two premier shortstops, or one of the nine left out in the cold, scrambling to make a deal before one of the other eight does? One seller, nine buyers – we know where the power lies.

Value Creation

When such inequities exist, these are the instances where value creation occurs. The value is less a function of your stellar ability to find bargains during the draft than it is your ability to manipulate the demand for particular players. You put yourself into the power position and nine other owners into a highly competitive position. If you are adroit at playing one offer against another without alienating your trading partners, you will receive more value in return than you would under normal trading conditions. Remember, you set the conditions, so you create the value with your strategy.

When you are thinking up strategies, think about how they can create value for you and cause your opponents to pay a premium to achieve their goals. If this is your minimum criteria for implementing a strategy, you should do just fine.

Which team would your competitors bet on to win? Why?

_____
_____
_____
_____
_____

What will differentiate your team from the others?

_____
_____
_____
_____
_____

Chapter 4. Valuation

Valuation

Player valuation is important. It just should not be your only strategy heading into the season. From a competitive standpoint, you know that your opponents will be looking for bargains as well. It is simply unlikely that you will gain much of an advantage on the other owners because of your ability to evaluate players better than they can. Evaluating players is an inexact science and anyone who claims that it is either is lying to you or is delusional. You should view player valuation as something you do not to lose as opposed to something you do that will win you the league.

What is the difference? If your system for valuing players is clearly wrong and completely different from every other team's system, your team will have no chance at winning. If you start the bidding for Cesar Izturis at $42, your team will suffer. That much is certain. On the other hand, if your dollar values for players are the most accurate in your league, you still might not win. During the draft, your opponents will bid more than you are willing to pay for some of the players you want. You can pass on those players until you find a bargain, but you can still end up with a suboptimal team. If the other teams in your league all undervalue speed, but overvalue power, should you necessarily fill all of your positions with speed players? You might be better off paying an extra dollar for a power player instead of paying a dollar less on another speed player. The price you pay for players does not happen in a vacuum. What others do will and should have some affect on what you do.

You should not be overly concerned with getting your valuation of players perfect; you should simply do your best not to get it wrong. So how do you get things wrong when doing your valuations? The

Fantasy Baseball Strategy

number one way people value players incorrectly is by not adjusting their valuations to the scoring of their league.

There are several sources of information available to the inquisitive fantasy baseball owner. The Internet offers free projections as well as statistics from previous years. There are also magazines that hit the newsstands every year that make projections, but also assign a dollar value to each player. Those dollar values never reflect actual dollar values in my league.

Every league is different. To reflect the desires of those who have played in it over the years, there are slight differences between my league and the standard leagues on which the magazines and websites make their projections. The same is probably true of your league. You have to realize that any change, however slight, will throw off the accuracy of those dollar values.

You have to realize that any change, however slight, will throw off the accuracy of those dollar values.

Your league may have fewer reserves. It may have fewer starters, or more statistical scoring categories. Your valuation of players should account for these factors.

Most fantasy owners account for the differences by adjusting on the fly using a combination of intuition and guestimation. This is usually what most owners do. If you have the desire to figure out a more objective system for rating players in your league, it might be a worthwhile exercise so you know in what ways your league differs from your normal valuation sources.

48　Valuation

Commonly Used Resources

One note about commonly used projections and dollar amount estimates: Since everyone else is going to use them, it would be helpful to know how they are likely to value players. You should at least familiarize yourself with a few of these readily available sources, so you have a little bit of competitive intelligence. Keep in mind that you need to make adjustments to account for differences in your league. Here are a few resources and some of the pitfalls of blindly following their recommendations:

One excellent source for ranking players is the *Player Rater on the ESPN.com* website. This is a good starting point for comparing players to each other. The method they use compares each player against the league averages in each scoring category. For instance, if a player hit the same amount of home runs as the average player, his category score would be 0.00. If he hit more his score would be positive and less if he hit less. The more he hits than the average, the higher the positive score. It is a quick and accessible resource for evaluating players.

The average player in the Major Leagues is not the average player in your draft.

What the *Player Rater* does not provide is how much you should spend on a given player. One key element that you should consider before you attempt to equate the *Player Rater* too literally with dollar values in your league is that the average player in the Major Leagues is not the average player in your draft. There are 30 Major League teams with 25 players on each roster. Most fantasy leagues only have 10, maybe 12 teams. Since there are approximately three times as

Fantasy Baseball Strategy

many players in the Majors as there are in most leagues, the average player in most leagues will be much better than the average player used in the *Player Rater*.

The *RotoTimes* has a system where you can enter in some of your league specifications and it will generate valuations. *USA Today* uses this system on their website as well. While the concept is good, it demonstrates how impossible it is for a magazine or website with thousands of readers to come up with a generic one size fits all projection system. My league has reserve players and the system does not adjust the values to account for them. Obviously, you are going to spend more on your starters than your reserves. It values players as if the statistics for all players on your team counted the same in the scoring– which they do not. There is also a drop down list for you to select your preferred hitter/pitcher split. This is the ratio of your budget allocated between hitting and pitching. The available choices range between 155:105 and 190:70. They must assume no one would ever want to spend more than 40% of their budget on pitching. I often spend more than 50% of my budget on pitching and have won my league five years out of the 10 we have played. Is this some sort of an anti-pitching conspiracy? It probably is not a conspiracy, but the parameters may be excluding certain strategies that can be effective in your league.

I suppose they assume no one would ever want to spend more than 40% of their budget on pitching.

Another resource people in your league may use to evaluate players is the annual *Sports Illustrated*

Baseball Preview since it has such a large circulation. This issue ranks players using a completely different system. It ranks players in different categories. Sports Illustrated assigns the top home run hitter the number one ranking in that category. It ranks the player with the next most home runs second, and so on. Then it totals up the rankings for each category and rank the player with the lowest overall score at the top. This may be a legitimate way of ranking players for the casual baseball fan, but it does not compare players in accurate relative terms. The number one home run hitter is better than the number two home run hitter is, but the system does not incorporate by how much. The top home run hitter may have hit 20 more home runs than the second place hitter did. Fantasy owners need to account for that kind of information.

There are of course, many ranking systems available on the Internet and in magazines. Many make projections for the upcoming season. This can be helpful because they generally account for players who performed poorly the year before because of injury. Not all do, so be careful. They also speculate on the development of young players and new players. These systems may be off considerably with their predictions, but at least these special cases usually make it on your radar screen. Before you draft, know that resources such as the *Player Rater* reflect player performance from a single year. It may not accurately reflect the probable impact these special case players can have on your league. You do not want to go into the

These valuation systems may be off considerably with their predictions.

Fantasy Baseball Strategy 51

draft armed solely with statistics from the previous year.

USA Today's Sports Weekly publishes the results of the *League of Baseball Alternative Reality (LABR)* auction. This is a fantasy league made up of baseball writers and fantasy experts. This is a valuable resource because it gives you an example of how knowledgeable fantasy owners actually bid on players. The projections and analysis aside, this is how they place their bets with their fantasy dollars. It is sometimes informative to read the commentary about each pick. There is usually a summary of each round highlighting the reasoning or lack of reasoning behind the picks.

The last type of resource that most people use to devise their valuation system is news and analysis. Following the baseball news and reading the analysis of fantasy writers keeps you up to date since the projections you read may be dated. Most fantasy magazines need to finalize their content in December to make it available by the typical February 1 release date. The LABR league

The projections and analysis aside, this is how they place their bets with their fantasy dollars.

holds its draft before the season with enough time to publish the results. Since you will probably be drafting your own team a couple of weeks later, important developments may occur. *ESPN.com* is a good overall online resource. It has general baseball news as well as fantasy specific analysis by Eric Karabell. This is where you learn the stories behind the statistics. When you know the stories, you can make your own judgment on how they may affect the numbers.

Adjusting for your League

It can be beneficial to have your own take on player values. This could be nothing more than identifying the players you want ahead of time. Some sort of analysis that gives you insight few others have can give you an advantage.

When attempting to generate your own analysis, you can use projections that you can download off the Internet. More often than not, you can simply use the statistics from the previous season. These numbers are absolute. They are fact, free of anyone else's spin. Your analysis can answer questions you have about what happened the last year. There is too much involved in making projections for each player, and then assigning a dollar value on top of those guesses. Try to take the guesswork out of it and stick with the facts. Draw your own conclusions from those facts.

You should look for players that scored well in your league, according to your rules.

When preparing for the new season, you should be curious to know which players were the most valuable to a team in your league the previous year. That information is something you can come up with yourself. It is entertaining to see which players the fantasy magazines deem their "Fantasy Player of the Year", but it typically means little to your team's prospects. The winner is usually someone like Alex Rodriguez – big surprise. You should look for players that scored well in your league, according to your rules.

What you find will probably surprise you. Looking at a list of the top 30 or so players on your own list, take note of those players that you were surprised to see ranked as high as they were. If the players surprised you, they would almost certainly surprise the other owners in your league. That is of course, if they could see what you see. Do you remember the Fundamental Theorem of Fantasy Sports? This is your information about the hand you have to play that your opponents do not have. The likelihood of them managing their teams differently than the way they would if they could see your hand is great, because they have no clue about the information you now hold.

Valuation Methodology

Before going any further into the details of any one possible way to determine value, let me reiterate that absolute accuracy is not essential. You can be confident that this is the "correct" way to evaluate players, but you will have to make assumptions along the way. This exercise is to help you gain insight. It is not to determine what a player will go for at your draft. Players will go for whatever price the owners in your league decide to pay. You are looking for general insight into the areas that your league tends to overlook. You are crunching numbers, but you are also creating a story from those numbers. The story those numbers tell will be about the behavior trends of the people in your league. Human behavior is anything but an exact science.

In general, you can try to adjust your player valuations using the following methodology:

STEP 1: Obtain or create projections for all eligible players. You can also use statistics from the previous year to identify trends in your league.

STEP 2: In each statistical category, determine from past league results what it took to gain a point in the standings for each category.

STEP 3: In each statistical category, figure out how many points each player is worth compared to the average or replacement player in your league. Calculations will depend on the type of statistic – cumulative or percentage.

STEP 4: Rank all players in descending point value. Estimate how many players will be taken in the draft. Take this number of players from the top of your list of players. These are by definition the players with positive dollar value.

STEP 5: Subtract the point value of the best player not taken in the draft from the point value of every player. This gives you the marginal point value of every player and is directly proportional to the player's dollar value. To get dollar values, multiply the marginal point values by a constant such that the sum total is equal to the total dollars available to be spent in the draft.

Valuation Example

The following is an example of how you might apply the valuation methodology to a specific league. Do not take these numbers as literal. They will differ depending on your league and the actual results of your league standings. The historical numbers used come

Fantasy Baseball Strategy 55

from one of my past custom 12-team mixed 5x5 leagues. Since the main point of this exercise is adjusting valuations to your specific league, it makes sense to use a non-standard league as an example.

STEP 1: Obtain or create projections for all eligible players. You can also use statistics from the previous year to identify trends in your league.

This example draws from 2003 final player statistics. Using projections downloaded from the Internet may be more useful when preparing for your draft, but using actual numbers will be helpful in identifying relative bargains from previous drafts. Depending on what you are trying to achieve, the choice is yours.

STEP 2: In each statistical category, determine from past league results what it took to gain a point in the standings for each category.

Using historical league information, determine for each category how many units it would take to gain a point in the standings. It would certainly be helpful to have the final standings of your league for several years, but in this case, the 2003 standings of my league will suffice. If you do not have this information or you are new to the league, you will have to get the results from someone

A new owner does not have the same access to or knowledge of the league's history. He probably does not even know what to ask for.

else. If your league uses a popular online league administrator, any owner should be able to access such information. You can see how a new player might be at a disadvantage. Not only does he not have the same access to or knowledge of the league's history, he probably does not even know what to ask for – unless he has read this book. You can be as precise as you like, or as in this example, simply take the range and divide by the number of teams. The point distribution might look like the following table:

Table 3: HR Category point distribution

HR	PTS
267	12
263	11
262	10
254	9
247	8
243	7
240	6
234	5
229	3.5
229	3.5
216	2
208	1

You might want to discard the leaders and the laggers of each category as they do in ice skating or diving. A team may have been exceptionally good at one category and poor at all the others. Another team may have tried to punt a category and its score is far below the rest of the teams. In this case, there were no such outliers. The range of HRs was 267-208 = 59.

Therefore, it took approximately 59/12 = 4.92 HRs to gain a point in the standings for that category. You then do the same for each category. The point distribution ranges for each category might look like the following table:

Table 4: Point distribution ranges for all categories

CATEGORY	RANGE	UNITS/POINT
HR	59	5
BA	0.020	0.002
RBI	232	19
SB	61	5
R	208	17
ERA	1.12	0.09
WHIP	0.262	0.02
W	29	2
SV	55	5
K	441	37

STEP 3: In each statistical category, figure out how many points each player is worth compared to the average or replacement player in your league. Calculations will depend on the type of statistic – cumulative or percentage.

Now that you know what it takes to gain a point in each category, you can see how much each player would improve your standings in your league. Start with player statistics as in Table 5. You first want to find the category value of the average player in your league. Common leagues have 23 total players: 14 hitters and 9 pitchers. In this league, there are 12 teams and 11 starting offensive players count in the scoring for each team. Take the average of the top 132 players who will contribute to the scoring in my league. The typical rotisserie style team will have 168 players for a 12-team league. You repeat this process for each category and total the category points. When you sort everything out on your spreadsheet by total points, it will work out. Until you do the final sort though, the numbers will not be correct. For the purposes of this example, it would be unnecessarily tedious to describe the entire process.

Table 5: Player statistics

PLAYER NAME	AB	HR	RBI	SB	R	BA
Albert Pujols	591	43	124	5	137	0.359
Gary Sheffield	576	39	132	18	126	0.330
Alex Rodriguez	607	47	118	17	124	0.298
Todd Helton	583	33	117	0	135	0.359
Carlos Beltran	521	26	100	41	102	0.307
Barry Bonds	390	45	90	7	111	0.341

The average starting player in my league was worth:
- 0.290 Batting Average
- 23 Home Runs
- 85 RBI
- 11 Stolen Bases
- 87 Runs

These numbers may seem high. Most of that is league specific, but the numbers for the average player of the top 132 is always going to be different – probably higher - than if you took the average from the total year-end statistics for your league. This is because teams move reserves in and out. They make

Fantasy Baseball Strategy

transactions throughout the year. The best 132 players do not play every game for every team in my league. You do not know who the best 132 players are until after the season.

Next, divide the category points each player contributes by the average units it takes to gain one point in the standings. For instance, Albert Pujols hit 43 HRs in 2003. We know from Step 2 that every five HRs will likely be worth one point in the standings. The average player in my league hit 23 HR, so Pujols' marginal HR value was 20 HR over a likely replacement player. Since 20/5 = 4, Albert Pujols was worth four points in HRs. That means if you were able to replace an average player from a team in this specific league with Albert Pujols, that team would have gained four points in the standings for home runs. With a head-to-head league, you can do this exercise the same way. You do not know what will happen in any given week, but you can still compare the cumulative statistics. You could conclude that an average team that added Pujols would have been 33% more likely to win the HR category each week. Table 6 shows the category points each player would have been worth.

Table 6: Cumulative category points

PLAYER NAME	HR PTS	RBI PTS	SB PTS	R PTS
Albert Pujols	4.1	2.0	-1.1	2.9
Gary Sheffield	3.2	2.4	1.4	2.2
Alex Rodriguez	4.9	1.7	1.2	2.1
Todd Helton	2.0	1.7	-2.1	2.7
Carlos Beltran	0.6	0.8	6.0	0.8
Barry Bonds	4.5	0.3	-0.7	1.4

Valuation

You will notice that batting average (BA) was left out of the table. Since BA is a percentage and not a cumulative statistical category, you have to do some additional calculations. It is important that you do this to get a more realistic measure of the impact a player has on your team batting average. This kind of calculation will help you answer the question, "Who would mean more to a fantasy team's batting average, Gary Sheffield with his .330 BA over 576 AB or Barry Bonds with his .341 BA over only 390 AB?" Good question, isn't it? To answer that question, you have to determine how many points each player is likely to increase your team's BA using the following formula:

$$= ((10/11)*1697) +H)/ ((10/11)*5947 +AB) -0.290)$$

Where did the numbers in this formula come from? The average team in my league had a team BA of .279. The average team had 1,697 hits over 5,947 AB.

Who would mean more to a fantasy team's batting average, Gary Sheffield with a .330 BA over 576 AB or Barry Bonds with a .341 BA over only 390 AB?

You can find this information by totaling the hits and AB from your league and then taking the average. The .290 BA of the average starting player was used for comparison in this example. As explained previously, this number is significantly higher than my actual league average. You can easily use the .279 number if you prefer that comparison better. My league happens to score 11 offensive players. When trying to determine a specific player's contribution to

Fantasy Baseball Strategy 61

BA, you have to remove the player he is replacing. This is where the 10/11 number comes from. You then simply add in the player's hits and AB to the other 10 players and subtract the BA of the average team. The results for our sample of players follow:

Table 7: Player BA contribution to average team

PLAYER NAME	AB	HITS	BA UNITS	BA PTS
Albert Pujols	591	212	0.0068	4.1
Gary Sheffield	576	190	0.0038	2.3
Alex Rodriguez	607	181	0.0008	0.5
Todd Helton	583	209	0.0067	4.1
Carlos Beltran	521	160	0.0015	0.9
Barry Bonds	390	133	0.0034	2.1

    To answer the question posed earlier, Gary Sheffield and Barry Bonds meant about the same to the average team's BA, adding between 0.0034 and 0.0038. Having one of these two on a team would bump it up two places in the standings for BA. Sheffield was actually slightly more valuable than Bonds was because he accounted for a greater percentage of his fantasy team's total ABs and Hits.

    You might be wondering now if the resources you have been basing your valuations on all these years take into account At Bats. If you do not know, you are not alone in your league. Valuation services rarely *Why would valuation services make their methodologies public when very few people care or bother to ask?* make their methodologies public. Why would they give away their "secrets" when very few people care or bother to ask? That gives you an idea of the kind of blind faith fantasy owners typically put into someone else's valuations. After you have finished learning the "secret" of valuing players specifically to your league from reading this chapter, you will know exactly what is accounted for in your player valuations.

Now that you have accurately determined how many BA points each player contributes to a team, you can add up the points for each category to determine the player totals. Your spreadsheet might look a bit like Table 8:

Table 8: Player Points

PLAYER NAME	HR PTS	RBI PTS	SB PTS	R PTS	AVG PTS	TOT PTS
Albert Pujols	4.1	2.0	-1.1	2.9	4.1	11.9
Gary Sheffield	3.2	2.4	1.4	2.2	2.3	11.7
Alex Rodriguez	4.9	1.7	1.2	2.1	0.5	10.4
Todd Helton	2.0	1.7	-2.1	2.7	4.0	8.3
Carlos Beltran	0.6	0.8	6.0	0.8	0.9	9.1
Barry Bonds	4.5	0.3	-0.7	1.4	2.1	7.4

You will have to make similar adjustments for pitching categories such as ERA and WHIP to account for innings pitched (IP). You can put together your own spreadsheet, but it will take you several hours. You can purchase the ***Adaptive Valuation Spreadsheet*** at www.fantasybaseballstrategy.com for a nominal fee. It will allow you to plug in variables according to the specifics of your league history. Innings pitched is an important statistic for determining the value of pitchers. The nature of pitching is different from hitting. In hitting, you can have several outstanding players and

Fantasy Baseball Strategy 63

still have holes in your lineup. You may have to play a backup catcher as your fantasy teams' starting catcher. He will not help you much in HR, SB, R, or RBI, and he will not have enough AB to hurt your average much. On the other hand, if you have a lousy pitcher on your fantasy staff, he not only does not help your team in some categories, he will actually make your team worse in ERA and WHIP. A poor pitcher on your staff will undo some of the work of a good pitcher. Innings pitched is like a multiplier. If the pitcher is good, you want more IP. If he is poor, you want fewer IP. It is probably better to pick up a middle reliever who rarely plays than to keep running out a lousy starting pitcher who eats up the innings.

You might think you are paying for the fourth best player in the draft; when in reality, you are only getting the fifth best.

You still have to assign the dollar values, which will be proportional to the point values. In other words, the player with the highest point value will also have the highest dollar value. An interesting note is that the original order of the players listed was sorted by the dollar values assigned by a prominent Internet source. The point totals do not quite correspond with the Internet source's dollar values after adjusting for the league. In practical terms, if you do not adjust for your league, you might think you are paying for the fourth best player in the draft; when in reality, you are only getting the fifth best.

STEP 4: Rank all players in descending point value. Estimate how many players will be taken in the draft. Take this number of players from the top of your list of players. These are by definition the players with positive dollar value.

You will have point values for pitchers and hitters. This league drafts 12 teams, each with 27 players. That means that the first 324 players drafted will have a positive dollar value. Every other player will be available in free agency. Therefore, those players are not allocated money from the overall draft budget. This step is very straightforward for non-keeper leagues where you know exactly how many players will be drafted. In keeper leagues, you will have to subtract keepers from the total. If you will not know which players will be keepers ahead of time, your spreadsheet might become complicated accounting for the variables.

After you sort the hitters and the pitchers by total point value, you will have an accurate ranking of the best players for your league. You still have one more step to come up with dollar values.

STEP 5: Subtract the point value of the best player not taken in the draft from the point value of every player. This gives you the marginal point value of every player and is directly proportional to the player's dollar value. To get dollar values, multiply the marginal point values by a constant such that the sum total is equal to the total dollars available to be spent in the draft.

After determining the subset of players that should be drafted – in this example 324 – determine how many hitters will be picked and how many pitchers will be picked. In some leagues, this number is set. You may know that every team will draft 14 hitters and 9 pitchers. Other leagues may be more flexible. You have to make an assumption in these cases. The 325th best player should be available as a free agent, so he represents the alternative to a player drafted. If you assume a 60:40 split, use the point value of the 195th best hitter, and the 130th best pitcher. You are interested in the marginal difference between a player you plan to pick at the draft and one who you could pick up after the draft.

To assign dollar values to players, you need to determine the total league budget. Typically, leagues allocate $260 to each team. In a 12-team league, the total budget is $260x12 = $3,120. You can then assign an allocation for dollars to hitters and to pitchers. You could use 60:40 for this case as well. Then you take the total of the marginal point values for the drafted players. Divide that total by each player's marginal value, and you get a percentage. Multiply each player's percentage times the total budget for hitting, and then for pitching, and you have the dollar amount for each player.

Finding the Right Mix

You have now completed an evaluation of individual players. Once you have created a spreadsheet[8] that adjusts player values to your league, you will have a list of players to examine. This will give you a great idea of what your team will need to look like in order to win. You can start mixing and

---

[8] Visit www.fantasybaseballstrategy.com for help designing a league-specific valuation spreadsheet.

66 **_Valuation_**

matching players to put together a mock team. Using your spreadsheet, you can cut and paste players into your team and total up the sum of their contributions. Then you can compare your hypothetical team to what it took to win each category of your league the previous year. You may find it difficult to get to 100% in every category with your draft alone. Luckily, you have all year to trade.

You have to balance affordability with overall production. It will be like putting together a puzzle. After doing this for a while, trying out all sorts of combinations, you will start to see patterns in your league's collective valuation of players.

Adding Up the Points

Table 9 shows you how you might compare players. You will notice that the sum of the five categories do not add up to the marginal point total. This is because the replacement player that each is compared to has a negative point value. A replacement player is one who was deemed unworthy of being drafted. He was not worth even spending $1 on. In this league, Garrett Anderson is worth 11.5 category points more than the average reserve player is.

Table 9: Roster talent mix tradeoffs

NAME	$	MAR PTS	HR	SB	R	RBI	AVG
I Suzuki	$24	12.7	-2.0	4.6	1.4	-1.2	1.5
G Anderson	$22	11.5	1.2	-0.9	-0.4	1.6	1.6
A Jones	$22	11.4	2.6	-1.3	0.8	1.6	-0.8
C Crawford	$21	10.9	-3.7	8.7	-0.4	-1.6	-0.6
S Sosa	$21	10.8	3.5	-2.1	0.7	0.9	-0.6

Fantasy Baseball Strategy

If you look at your previous year's league standings, you can see how many category points it would have taken to jump one place in the overall standings. In my league, the winning team had 90 category points and the worst team has 40 points. With 12 teams, four points was worth about one place in the standings. That means that if all the teams were relatively equal, adding Garrett Anderson to one of them would be worth about three spots in the standings.

Suppose you have filled out most of your key roster spots and have about $20 left for one more impact outfielder. How do you choose? It depends on your other players. At opposite ends of the spectrum are Carl Crawford and Sammy Sosa. Crawford gives you plenty of SB, but he actually is below average in everything else, especially HR. Sosa is a slugger through and through and home runs are his strength. There are definite tradeoffs for each player. Perhaps Andruw Jones is a good compromise since he has power and although he did not steal much last year, he is still known as a speedy defender. He could start stealing again.

It is probably best to determine what kind of category strength your core team already has so you will know which attributes to look for in a player.

It is probably best to determine what kind of roster category strength your core team already has so you will know which attributes to look for in a player. You might already know what you are starting with if you are in a keeper league. Maybe you simply have players who you think will have big years and want to make sure you get them. Once you have an idea about your core roster, you can determine whom else you might want to add. Let us say your core roster looks like this one in Table 10:

Table 10: Roster category strength

NAME	$	MAR PTS	HR	SB	R	RBI	AVG
J Edmonds	$18	9.4	3.2	-1.9	0.1	0.2	-0.7
L Berkman	$18	9.4	0.4	-1.1	1.3	0.4	-0.1
O Cabrera	$20	10.5	-1.2	2.6	0.4	-0.2	0.4
Total	$57	29.3	2.4	-0.4	1.8	0.4	-0.3

Some quick roster analysis of the core players you want to start the season off with indicates that you need SB and AVG the most. Of the five players in Table 9, Ichiro Suzuki seems to fit the bill the best. He would provide strength in your team's two weakest areas. You have many alternatives. You could try to draft Crawford and concentrate on AVG for the rest of the draft. Maybe, you think speed will come cheap and Garrett Anderson is the better choice. At least you are making informed decisions. Having the ability to make this kind of analysis can be very valuable.

Much as the Oakland Athletics, chronicled in the book *Moneyball*[9], zeroed in on on-base percentage as the most undervalued measure of a player's real-life baseball contribution, you too will find scoring categories that are relatively undervalued in your league. You might find that owners do not pay much attention to Runs or WHIP. Maybe they seem to pay excessively for categories such as HRs or AVG. These

---

[9] Lewis, M. *Moneyball*. New York, NY. W.W. Norton & Company

Fantasy Baseball Strategy

discoveries are invaluable to you when planning your team. You will have to make tradeoffs. Just as the A's would like to have more money to work with, you will wish you had more as well. Luckily, there is probably a salary cap in your league, so there will be no teams like the Yankees to worry about. Your budget constraint is mandated and you must play within those confines. While you are consciously making tradeoffs, taking into account your league's collective tendencies, your competition will be handing you productive players – important pieces to completing your puzzle – at bargain prices.

To save you some frustration, here is a little secret. If you think there will be a magic combination of players that will put you at the top of every category, you are mistaken. It is almost a certainty that you will not be able to draft a winning team that gives you 100% of what you need across the board. Keep in mind that throughout the year you will pick up free agents and make trades. Your hope is that you will make smart trades that improve your team. You have to realize that your team is far from complete at the end of draft day. Ideally, your team will incrementally improve as the season progresses.

If you think there will be a magic combination of players that will put you at the top of every category, you are mistaken.

Accounting for Reserves

You may want to make one more adjustment. With your $260, you need to draft an entire team, which probably includes reserve players that do not contribute

Valuation

to your final statistics much, if at all. If you draft optimally and your starters are indeed your best players, barring injury, your reserve players should never count in the scoring. If you decide to use the valuation method described earlier in this chapter, reserves were already accounted for. The example assumed that you would spend the minimum on reserve players or they had little to no value. You can change those assumptions by increasing the range of players from which you take your averages.

If you decide that doing your own valuations is too much work for you, and simply want to use published valuations, you can still adjust for reserves. In fact, you really should, because the valuation services cannot account for which players will be your team's starters and which ones will be your reserves. You may have to adjust your valuations by more than 30%. This method will not be completely accurate, but neither will your valuations. It is still better than not adjusting at all.

Valuation services cannot account for which players will be your team's starters and which ones will be your reserves. You may have to adjust your valuations by more than 30%.

You will have to make a decision about how much to weigh the contributions of starting players versus the contributions of reserve players. The actual weight does not matter too much since you will compare all players on a relative basis. It will have an effect on your final dollar amounts though. The average team that drafts 27 players for $260 has $9.63 to spend for each player on average. It does not make sense to

Fantasy Baseball Strategy

spend the same amount on your reserves as you spend on your starters, does it? Let us say you will spend $3 on each of the nine reserve players you will draft. That means you have $233 to spend on 18 starters. The average starter should be worth $12.94, not $9.63, as he would be if you evenly distributed your money among all players on your roster, including reserves. You can use this as a multiplier 12.94/9.63 = 1.34 to account for greater emphasis on your projected starters. This means that if you spend $3 on each of your nine reserves, you will have $60 extra to spend on your starters. Those $60 spread out over 18 starters is equal to $3.31 more per starter. On average, you will have 34% more to spend on your starters, which is quite significant.

Where to Find Bargains

The value of determining dollar values can be much more that having a sheet of paper that tells you which players to draft. You can infer valuable draft intelligence that gives you information about round dynamics and the best times to find bargains. You can do this by comparing the actual values of players you just computed with the amount people paid for players in the previous draft. For example, take the draft order and dollar amounts of your league's latest draft, and compare it to the final year-end statistics. This will

Determining dollar values allows you to obtain draft intelligence about round dynamics and the best time to find bargains.

show you were the relative bargains were in the draft. Projections will also work in lieu of the final statistics because they reflect the change in player value. It may

72 *Valuation*

be necessary to clean the data in a spreadsheet or database to correlate actual performance to dollars spent. You can then see which rounds allowed owners to stretch their buying power the most. A visual breakdown of you results might look like Figure 1.

Figure 1: When in the draft to find values

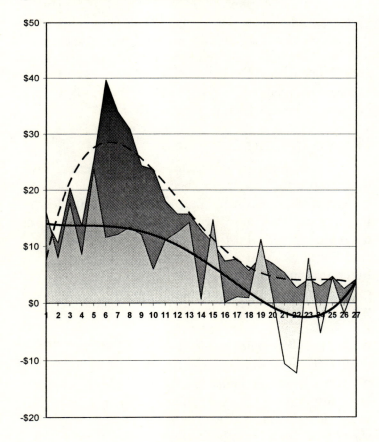

Fantasy Baseball Strategy

The dark area shows the average price of players per round in my league draft. The lighter area represents the actual earned values of those players. The dotted trend line illustrates the movement in draft prices as the rounds go by. The first five rounds are lower because teams each team could keep five players (Keepers) from the year before for a nominal increase in price. The solid black trend line represents the actual year-end values of players. Each round refers to 12 players bid on as each owner gets a turn to name a player for bid.

The Draft is Only Half the Battle

The first thing that should stand out to you is that the actual values are significantly lower than the draft values. Does that mean the valuations people use are too high? Probably not. More likely, it reflects the fact that there were many players drafted that were injured or severely underperformed. These players brought down the actual earned figures significantly. For instance, Randy Johnson was probably one of the most expensive draft choices at the 2003 draft, but ended up being only the 750th best player and worth a crushing -$8.50 to the average team in this particular league. There are no upside surprises that can offset a $50 shortfall in expected performance. The same can be said of Shawn Green, Jason Giambi, Brian Giles, or Vladimir Guerrero who disappointed mightily after being drafted for very high prices. Also, players who

This chart should be a powerful reminder to you that the draft is not your season. It shows that the draft is only 52% of your season!

were not drafted, but ended up contributing significantly throughout the season are not reflected.

This chart should be a powerful reminder to you that the draft is not your season. It tells you that you will draft players that perform much worse than you expected. It also should tell you that trading, free agency, competitive strategy, and roster moves play a tremendous role in determining your team's fate in the league. How much of a difference do they make? The actual earned value of players drafted in this league was only 52% of their cost at the draft. In other words, the draft is only half of your season! If this is the only thing you take away from this book, you will still be ahead of most fantasy baseball owners who believe their fate is inextricably linked to the draft. You can make mistakes in the draft and still recover.

Intelligent Drafting

The first five rounds represent keeper players. As expected, these rounds represent some of the highest actual performance per draft dollar spent. What it should point out though is that while there will obviously be some players who are great bargains, keepers are far from guaranteed. In fact, keepers still underperformed on average. Most keepers will be bargains, but a few will greatly disappoint.

Round 6 of this draft is essentially the beginning of the auction for non-keeper leagues. From there to Round 10, the chart shows that owners severely overpay for players in this league. The best players are usually put up for bid in these rounds. The trend lines begin to converge between Round 11 and 19. Values can be found in this timeframe of the draft. An important point to keep in mind is just because people

Fantasy Baseball Strategy

overbid in the early rounds, you should not necessarily wait until Round 11 to pick up your first player. The prices do decline significantly in these middle rounds, but so do the actual earned values of players. At Round 19, the actual values go negative.

A player that earns $0 is no better or worse than a non-drafted free agent is. Players picked up between Rounds 20 through 26 would have hurt the teams that drafted them. They turned out to be worse than the average player was. This should be a warning sign that while players are inexpensive, many are simply not worth drafting. At the very end of the draft, there is a noticeable up tick in value. This looks to be where teams have filled most of their roster spots and begin to speculate on potential keepers or minor league phenoms. Notice that the prices actually increase going into the final round. This indicates that owners save up their final dollars for that one player they have been waiting for. Knowing the dynamics of the final eight rounds might lead you to a strategy that limits your bidding activity after the 19th round and raises it again during the final two.

If you decide to do a similar analysis for your specific league, you can gain some valuable insights about the draft behavior of your competition. You will also be able to understand the tradeoff between a cheap player you can pick up at the draft, and someone you can pick up as a free agent more easily. At certain points during the draft, it will be clearer that you should pass on a marginal player because he is not obviously better than any old replacement player is. Even if you decide to forgo this exercise yourself, remember that half of your team's points will probably come from players you did not even draft. Write that down.

Valuation

How much of your team's scoring will come from the draft?

How will you adjust the player values for your league?

How will you determine the optimal mix of players for your team?

Where will you find bargains in your draft?

Chapter 5. Special Considerations

Special Considerations

Before you draft, you should be aware of special circumstances that may affect the players you select. This chapter could very well have gone under the valuation umbrella, but it is separated out to avoid confusion with individual player valuation.

The Under Appreciated

In most leagues, pitchers are worth more than hitters are. To be more accurate, good pitchers are worth more than good hitters. Pitching tends to be severely undervalued. The fantasy experts often suggest spending a minimum of 60% of your money on hitting, and a maximum of 40% of it on pitching, even though pitching counts for half of the scoring.

In most leagues, 14 hitters and only 9 pitchers count towards scoring. Simple math shows that you have 55% more hitters to produce your offensive statistics. The actual ratio of players who are hitters vs. pitchers is 61:39. Perhaps this is where the dollar allocation comes from. This line of reasoning is completely wrong though. Since there are fewer pitchers and 50% of the scoring comes from pitching, the average price of pitchers should be more than the average price of hitters.

The average price of pitchers should be more than the average price of hitters.

This of course is hardly ever the case in most drafts because virtually every fantasy resource available has drilled the opposite into our heads. That does not mean that you should necessarily spend 50% of your money on pitching. What it does mean is that you should know that 50% of your points come from pitching, so spend your money wisely on quality pitchers. If you make a mistake on a pitcher, the impact is greater.

Allocation of Dollars and Sense

If 50% of the fantasy points in your league come from pitching, why would so many experts advocate such a weighting towards hitting? It makes very little sense.

Think of roster allocation in business terms because as a fantasy owner, you are essentially pretending to be a General Manager of a baseball team. General Managers need to consider baseball from a business perspective. Look at these arguments from that perspective for a little bit. Suppose you are the General Manager of a company that officially licenses professional sports uniforms.

You have two lines of clothing, baseball and basketball. Each clothing division submitted you a $10 million budget based on projections from an independent market research company. How do you allocate your dollars? Details of the revenue breakdown follow:

Figure 2: Uniform company financial report

BASKETBALL UNIFORMS	%	ENDORSEMENT COST	ESTIMATED SALES
James	64%	$6,400,000	$9,920,000
Anthony	26%	$2,600,000	$4,030,000
O'Neil	6%	$600,000	$930,000
Garnett	4%	$400,000	$620,000
TOTAL	100%	$10,000,000	$15,500,000

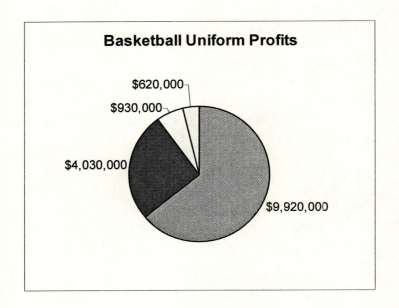

Basketball Uniform Profits

BASEBALL UNIFORMS	%	ENDORSEMENT COST	ESTIMATED SALES
Bonds	22%	$2,222,222	$3,222,222
Giambi	19%	$1,944,444	$2,819,444
Prior	17%	$1,666,667	$2,416,667
Martinez	14%	$1,388,889	$2,013,889
Johnson	11%	$1,111,111	$1,611,111
Pujols	8%	$833,333	$1,208,333
Rodriguez	6%	$555,556	$805,556
Ichiro	3%	$277,778	$402,778
TOTAL	100%	$10,000,000	$14,500,000

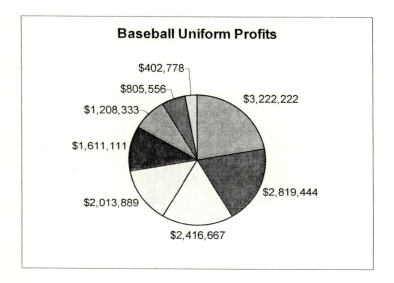

If you are confused, that is the point. All the numbers and charts make this exercise look like something out of a business school class. With so much information in front of you, it is easy to give up and let the "experts" take over as you say to yourself, "Just tell me what I need to know." People want to have someone translate what it all means to them, even if all it takes is a little common sense to find the answer. It is only natural. As an advanced fantasy baseball owner, you cannot afford to rely on what an expert is telling 2 million other people. Experts trying to advocate the dollar values they came up with have to generalize. They sell more that way. You have to rely on your own common sense to determine what applies to your situation and what does not. The point is, look past all the unnecessary complexity, the names, the dollar amounts, and the percentages, and focus on what is important.

82 *Special Considerations*

The answer to how you would allocate your money is simple. You would put your money where the overall company can make the most profits. In the section about where to find bargains in the draft, you looked at where you could get the most performance value per dollar. In this case, profit is your performance value. It is the bottom line. If you can make a higher profit by allocating more money to the areas that offer you a better performance value per dollar ratio, you ought to do it. Does it make much sense to do otherwise? In our hypothetical company's case, you can make $0.55 of profit for each dollar spent on basketball endorsements, but only $0.45 for baseball endorsements. It certainly makes sense to consider allocating more dollars towards basketball. There may be other considerations, but they are all subordinate to the bottom line. See past the superfluous arguments and focus on what really counts.

Some legitimate considerations why you would not dump baseball uniforms in favor of selling only basketball uniforms might be:

- You do not want to risk relying on just a few products (diversification).
- Endorsement profits are cyclical and baseball may be in favor next year.
- Baseball and basketball seasons do not run simultaneously.

These are all important considerations for keeping a balanced mix. Still, if you were going to favor one or the other, wouldn't you pick the one that gives you the greatest profits? Certainly, just because you have twice as many baseball uniforms as you do basketball, a 2:1 dollar allocation in favor of baseball uniforms would not make sense. Stick to what gets you to the bottom line!

Common Arguments Refuted

Common sense dictates that you should allocate dollars in correlation to the value players contribute. The arguments you hear for hitters over pitchers should merit your consideration, but they should still be subordinate to the performance per dollar argument. Here are some of the arguments in favor of hitters over pitchers along with responses to them:

1. You need to draft more hitters than pitchers.

So what? You can divide your money between hitters and pitchers fairly equally. Then you spend a little less per hitter than you would per pitcher. In the business example, the James basketball uniform is worth the most to your company so you compensate him the most. If pitchers give you a better performance to dollar ratio, then spend relatively more per pitcher. If hitters offer you a better ratio in your league, spend more per hitter. It is simple, go where the bargains are available.

2. Everyone values hitters more than pitchers so you will just waste your money if you allocate more to pitchers.

Ridiculous. Just because you are aware that pitching categories mean as much as hitting categories in your league, you will not instantly become a fool in every other way. You will obtain better pitchers who mean more to your team's overall performance than mediocre hitters will. It is actually extremely advantageous to you that other teams favor hitters so much. You will get more "bang for your buck". The most important thing to know is that when you win the bidding for a pitcher, you will only be bidding $1 more than someone else is willing to pay. Spending 20% more on your pitching staff does not equate to spending 20% more per pitcher. You only pay marginally more for your pitchers. It is not as if you will be wildly overpaying for each one. If your league does not value pitchers as they should value them, then you will have less competition when bidding and end up with the pitchers you want.

When you win the bidding for a pitcher, you will only be bidding $1 more than someone else is willing to pay.

3. You will be stuck with great pitching but lousy hitting.

Have they ever heard of trading? Do not worry too much about your dollar allocation between pitchers and hitters right after the draft. You have all season to reallocate by trade and free agency. Assume you spend 50% of your money on pitchers and no one in your league spends more than 40%. Your pitchers will be the best or at least very strong, and your hitting will be relatively weak. Great! You will be the first person the other owners call when they need to trade for a pitcher. They will have little choice of with whom they can trade. You on the other hand will get to choose from the entire league. That is trading power.

Remember that self-interest wins out. Others will probably tell you that pitchers are not worth as much as hitters are. They will probably even believe it themselves. Nevertheless, if they can obtain a player – even a pitcher - that will help them separate from the pack, they will pay a premium for him. They will have to trade with you no matter how much more they love hitters.

Even if you find it difficult to trade, at the very least you will have a dominant pitching staff. On draft day, you almost assured yourself of finishing in the top half of your league no matter how bad your hitters are. Five or six teams in your league cannot say the same. It should be comforting to know that your draft was worth an advantage of at least five slots in the standings. You still have the entire season to wheel and deal so you can shift those performance/dollar draft values to your hitters.

4. Pitcher performance is less predictable than hitter performance.

That could be true if you are comparing average pitchers against average hitters. If you are able to draft quality pitchers for less than they are worth, you should be able to predict quite accurately, how well they will perform. In addition, some pitchers and pitching categories are easier to predict than hitters and hitting categories. If he stays healthy, wouldn't you expect Randy Johnson to get you quite a few strikeouts? Without a doubt, you would!

5. Pitchers get injured more than hitters do.

Not true. People take for granted that pitchers get injured more often than hitters are. The evidence shows that pitchers are in fact less likely to go on the Disabled List (DL) than hitters are. In a 2001 article[10]

---

[10] Conte, S., Regua, R., Garrick, G., *Disability Days in Major League Baseball.* American Journal of Medicine, July 2001.

86 Special Considerations

for the *American Journal of Sports Medicine* by Stan Conte, head trainer of the San Francisco Giants, he provides injury data for 11 MLB seasons from 1989 to 1999. He found that pitchers accounted for 48.4% of the injury list reports. That means hitters accounted for 51.6% or 1,692 DL reports.

Table 11: Number of DL reports per position

Type	DL Reports	No. of Players in 2003	Players over 11 yrs*	Reports per Player
Pitchers	1,590	611	6,721	23.7%
Hitters	1,692	552	6,072	27.9%
C	251	90	990	25.4%
1B	176	59	649	27.1%
2B	202	70	770	26.2%
3B	166	63	693	24.0%
SS	249	59	649	38.4%
OF	648	211	2,321	27.9%

In 2003, 611 pitchers played in the Major Leagues and 581 hitters played. Extrapolating those figures over 11 years to get an estimate of the total number of players at each position, Table 11 shows that pitchers actually go on the DL less than any other position in baseball! You can expect a 23.7% chance that any given pitcher will go on the DL each season. The average hitter is likely to go on the DL 27.9% of the time. If you are going to worry about the frequency of injuries,

An average pitcher has a 23.7% chance of going on the DL, while an average hitter has a 27.9% chance.

worry about your shortstops that go on the DL 38.4% of the time.

Now that you know pitchers are injured less frequently than hitters are, you probably want to know if their injuries tend to be more severe. Table 12 shows that in fact their injuries tend to keep them on the DL longer.

Table 12: Average days on DL

TYPE	TOTAL DL DAYS	PLAYERS	DAYS ON DL	AVG. STINT ON DL
Hitters	84,275	6,072	13.9	50
Pitchers	111,258	6,721	16.6	69
All	195,533	12,793	15.3	60

Pitchers spend an average of 16.6 days on the DL while hitters spend 13.9 days on it. Pitchers may be injured less frequently, but when they do visit the DL, they tend to stay longer. One factor to account for is that starting players become active when they are available while starting pitchers may have to wait for a decent time to join the rotation so they do not disrupt the other four starters.

Pitchers are hurt less frequently, but stay injured longer. You can plan strategies to optimize your pitching staff around that knowledge.

In summary, you should be concerned about injuries, but not necessarily more concerned about injuries to pitchers. Pitchers are hurt less frequently, but stay injured longer. You can plan strategies to optimize your pitching staff around that knowledge. Later in the

88   ***Special Considerations***

chapter, you will read about managing injuries among starting pitchers so you can reduce the risk.

Starters vs. Relievers

Many leagues require that of those few pitching roster spots, a certain number must be reserved for relievers. This means you have a limited amount of starting pitchers. Since starting pitchers generally throw two to three times as many innings as relievers, on a relative basis, their statistics are more meaningful in most categories. Starters generally will be superior in absolute categories such as Wins and Ks. Since ERA and WHIP are not absolute, you must consider them weighted averages.

Table 13 shows a starter with an ERA of 2.25 over 220 innings is far more valuable than a reliever with an ERA of 2.05 over 70 innings. How much more valuable is he? The ERAs are close, but the starter has over three times the innings pitched.

Table 13: Pitching staff with one superior starter

POS	ER	INN	ERA
SP*	*55*	*220*	*2.25*
SP	98	220	4.00
SP	98	220	4.00
SP	98	220	4.00
RP	27	70	3.50
RP	27	70	3.50
RP	27	70	3.50
Team	**430**	**1090**	**3.55**

The starter is actually more valuable than you might think because he is giving you 220 innings at an

ERA far superior to the average replacement player. If you do not have a superior starter, you need to replace him with a different pitcher. The typical starter with an ERA of 4.00 will allow 98 runs over 220 innings as opposed to the superior starter's 55 runs allowed.

Table 14: Pitching staff with one superior reliever

POS	ER	INN	ERA
SP	98	220	4.00
SP	98	220	4.00
SP	98	220	4.00
SP	98	220	4.00
RP	27	70	3.50
RP	27	70	3.50
RP*	*16*	*70*	*2.05*
Team	462	1090	3.81

A good starter has a much greater impact on your team ERA than a good reliever. In this case, Table 14 indicates a 32 increase in earned runs by substituting a superior starter with a reliever. That translates into a 0.26 difference in ERA, which could be worth about three points in the standings.

You will probably have to consider budget constraints when choosing between drafting starters and relievers. Starting pitchers may very well be worth more than relievers, but they may also be more expensive. If you could substitute a superior starting pitcher with two or more superior relievers for the same price, you would have to consider the alternative. Table 15 shows how your pitching staff might look if you had three outstanding relievers instead of one superior starter.

Table 15: Pitching staff with three superior relievers

POS	ER	INN	ERA
SP	98	220	4.00
SP	98	220	4.00
SP	98	220	4.00
SP	98	220	4.00
RP*	16	70	2.05
RP*	16	70	2.05
RP*	16	70	2.05
Team	439	1090	3.62

This table demonstrates that the superior starter is worth more than having three superior relievers when it comes to ERA. The key concept here is if you do not have a certain player in your lineup, you must have a replacement player in his place. You must know how much this replacement will hurt your team statistics and have a plan for dealing with it. In the previous example, by choosing the excellent relief pitcher over the excellent starting pitcher, your team is 32 runs worse. How will you make that up?

One caveat is that when your league has very little depth, it may be wise to consider relievers who will not hurt your team as much as poor starters will. A superior starter accounts for a larger percentage of total innings pitched than a superior reliever. If your league chooses from only one league – AL or NL or a subset of a league, the last thing you want is to have several poor starters on your team. If you must have poor pitchers on your team because there are no alternatives, it is better to have poor relievers than poor starters. They simply will not hurt your team as much.

If your team needs more saves, you will need closers. Just realize that your primary reason for getting closers is for the saves, not the other categories. Premier closers can account for an overwhelming percentage of the saves you need to win that category. For that reason, they are indeed valuable. Just be aware of the other players you are giving up to get them. Consider picking up mediocre relief pitchers that get the saves for their team, and spending the difference somewhere else. You looked at ERA in the previous example, but a similar case for starting pitchers can be made in Wins, WHIP, and if you league counts them, Strikeouts. Good starters help you more in those categories. Good relievers help more in Saves.

One caveat is that when your league has very little depth, it may be wise to consider relievers who will not hurt your team as much as poor starters will.

Reality Check

You probably intuitively know that a good starter is more valuable than a good reliever is, but these examples show you just how much. You could calculate the expected impact each roster move has on your team, but for practical purposes, most people do not have the time or patience for that kind of analysis. It is probably enough just to know that, in general, a quality starter is significantly more valuable than a quality reliever is.

Eric Gagne and John Smoltz are fabulous fantasy players, but if you were more concerned about

ERA and WHIP than about Saves, Mark Prior or Jason Schmidt would be better choices for your team.

Managing for Starting Pitcher Injuries

The theory that pitchers sustain injuries more often than hitters do has been dispelled. When they do go on the DL though, they tend to stay on it longer. There are some things you, as a fantasy owner can do to minimize the injury risk by picking pitchers who will avoid long debilitating injuries.

It is possible you have heard the General Manager of your favorite baseball team say that pitchers get injuries too much. You have to question what that means. Too much for what? Does that mean they are injured more than hitters are, or does that mean that the team cannot afford to invest so much in a single pitcher for fear of injuries? From the typical Major League Baseball team's perspective, this may be the case. Few teams are like the Yankees and can afford to have a pitching staff with more than one ace. Most teams are lucky to have one legitimate ace – let us define an "ace" as one of the top 12 starting pitchers in the league – and if he were to be injured, the hopes of the entire team go down the drain. Injuries to starting pitchers are devastating to a MLB team simply because each one accounts for approximately 15-20% of his team's innings pitched. An injury to a hitter means you only have to replace $1/9^{th}$ of the team's plate appearances. General Managers are responsible for putting seats in the park all season long, not just when the team's ace is healthy. True aces

> *There are many things you, as a fantasy owner can do to minimize the injury risk.*

Fantasy Baseball Strategy

of course, also cost a lot more to sign. For these reasons, they prefer to diversify by signing four or five serviceable starters with less invested in aces.

This is not a bad strategy, and as a fantasy owner, you can take something away from this. If you invest in one ace, you are gambling that he will stay healthy all year long or at least until you trade him. A solid fantasy strategy is to have more than one very good pitcher so if one is injured; your team still has a chance. This is not Major League Baseball, but fantasy baseball. Unlike real baseball, middle relief is worth very little in most leagues. MLB teams hope to get a solid five or six innings from a decent starter, hand it over to two or three relievers, and if fortunate enough to have the lead, maybe the closer will get the ball. In fantasy baseball, your starters effectively hand the ball over to your closers. Your starters and closers will account for a greater percentage of pitching than they would on a MLB team, so they need to be solid pitchers.

In fantasy baseball, your starters effectively hand the ball over to your closers.

What is a solid pitcher though? Young pitchers with high pitch counts do get hurt because they have not had the time to condition their arms to the rigors of a Major League season. Veterans who have pitched 220 innings year in and year out can take it. How do you find those pitchers who can take it? It just so happens that the great pitchers in the game happen to be the ones who log the innings consistently. People do not consider pitchers great if they are always injured, or have not performed well regularly. Great pitchers come at a premium though.

Pitcher Characteristics

It is helpful to think of your pitching staff as a portfolio. You want to spread out the risk across your pitching staff. Each pitcher presents a series of tradeoffs that represent different levels of risk for the fantasy owner. It may be unrealistic to have a staff full of Cy Young caliber pitchers who consistently log 200+ innings a season with flawless mechanics. But you also do not want all your pitchers to be unproven players who have never gone more than 130 innings. Pitcher characteristics that do not necessarily show up in the statistics will have a real impact on your injury management.

Pitcher Type

There are four types of pitchers. Cy Young caliber pitchers are expected to be frontrunners for the league's top pitcher of the year award. All Stars are pitchers that have recently been named an All Star or have performed at that level. An average to solid starter is one who has the ability to win between 10 and 15 games each year. A below average starter is one whose performance thus far has not warranted playing time on your roster. It is clear which types of pitchers you would want, but if you already have a few All Stars on your team, you might consider some Below Average pitchers. You should ask yourself whether Below Average pitchers are that way because they lack talent, or because they have yet to put everything together. You do not want to miss the next Roy Halladay.

Type
Cy Young
All Star
Solid Starter
Below Average

Average Innings Pitched

When you are considering which pitchers to draft, you should pay close attention to the number of innings pitched over the previous years. Think of different plateaus that starting pitchers reach. Starting from the bottom, 130 innings seems to be the level at which pitchers become legitimate starters. Any amount less than that and perhaps the player could be a long reliever with occasional spot starter duty. Fantasy owners often make pitchers with this many innings and terrific statistics the object of their desire. They project their performances out to 220 innings and think they have made a great discovery. Keep in mind that relievers generally have better statistics than regular starters because lineups only see them once or twice per appearance.

Avg. IP
230+
200+
170+
130+

The number 170 is no magical number, but an indication that a player's team thinks of a player highly enough not to move him from the rotation to the bullpen and back. A player with this many innings has pretty well established himself in the rotation and you should see consistent playing time from him in the future. For young players with potential, 170 innings seems to be the point where they have proven to themselves that they can endure the rigors of a Major League season. After this point, without the pressure of trying to stay in the rotation, talented pitchers will often improve markedly in the following years.

The 200-inning level is the gold standard. Pitchers who consistently reach this level are usually considered their team's number one or two starter. Only on rare occasions will you see a starter with 200+ innings and very poor statistics. When you do see such a player, he usually plays for a lousy team, but still ranks as one of the team's leaders in victories. At 230 innings, you start to reach workhorse territory. This indicates that a pitcher goes deep into games, giving him a greater chance of picking up wins. These pitchers are great to have, but beware of those who have reached this level three years in a row. It could be a sign of overuse and a precursor to not only minor injuries, but also season-ending surgery.

If you want to study the effects of the number of innings and pitches thrown in detail, you can look up Pitcher Abuse Points. Trying to apply the formula to every player you might consider starts to get into the realm of analysis paralysis. If you have the patience, knock yourself out.

Seniority

The safest player in terms of seniority is the established veteran with a consistent Major League record. The next level of seniority is the Up and Comer. These are usually more talented players, phenoms who teams slate as the "future aces" of their teams. There is a lot riding on their health. Before they consider them established veterans, teams will baby them, keeping track of pitches, and will pull them as soon as they run into trouble to protect their fragile psyches. Be aware that these practices will limit the player's innings and reduce the amount of wins you might otherwise expect.

Seniority
Established Veteran
Up and Comer
Journeyman
Rookie

Journeymen who get hurt often do not last long in the league. Since teams usually do not have as much invested in them as established veterans or top prospects, teams occasionally call upon journeymen to "take one for the team". They may be bumped from a start, moved back a day, pitch long relief in a blowout, or be moved to the bullpen indefinitely. This increases the risk that you will not get what you expected when you drafted them.

Rookie starters are hard to predict. On occasion, you will have terrific performances by a rookie such as Dontrelle Willis or Brandon Webb, but these are rare. You probably never heard of them before their first Major League appearances, so teams do not coddle them like a Josh Beckett, or a Mark Prior. This more liberal approach may affect their follow-up performances negatively.

Mechanics

You do not have to be an expert on biomechanics, but you should be aware of how pitcher mechanics might affect a player's health. Players that throw with an ease of motion and a compact, no-nonsense delivery like Mark Prior should be able to avoid serious injuries better than pitchers with poor mechanics that put undue strain on the joints and tendons. If

Mechanics
Flawless
Clean
Unorthodox
Poor

you follow baseball, you will hear announcers comment on pitchers with good mechanics and pitchers with poor mechanics.

One sign of poor mechanics is when you see pitchers who change the way they throw throughout a game. It could be a signal that trouble is brewing. You have to question the reason why a pitcher would completely change the way he throws. In many cases, a pitcher has thrown a certain way since high school or even childhood. It does not seem as though a pitcher would willingly change the arm motion that has taken him to the Major Leagues, made him millions of dollars, and won him accolades for his performance unless something was very wrong. Usually, the only reason a pitcher would consciously change his throwing motion mid-season is if he has experienced discomfort or injury, and he is doing something to avoid foreseeable injury.

Pitching coaches do like to work on mechanics with pitchers. Most mechanical alterations will be hardly noticeable. They will probably be gradual changes too. You should be the most concerned about drastic changes in mechanics during the season. If you can see the difference without someone pointing it out to you, look out. At least it merits further investigation.

You might also see a pitcher drop down to throw from a "Laredo" position or some other arm angle during a game. While this may fool a hitter occasionally, it indicates a pitcher who experiments with his mechanics. A pitcher confident enough to throw a novelty pitch in a game has certainly practiced it a few times before. Pitchers that come to mind who have often changed the angle of their release points during a game are Orlando "El Duque" Hernandez, John Smoltz, and Kevin Brown. All three have experienced serious injuries that forced them to miss full seasons. All excellent pitchers in their primes, the consequences of poor habits tend to increase with age or in combination

Why would a pitcher willingly change the arm motion that has taken him to the Major Leagues?

with the other injury warning signs mentioned. You just want a pitcher who stays with what he does best, blowing away hitters.

Stuff

You often hear about a pitcher's stuff, which is the baseball term for the type and caliber of pitches he throws. All things being equal, you would rather have a pitcher with excellent stuff, a 95 mph fastball, nasty slider, split-finger fastball that falls off the table, and a changeup that looks exactly like his fastball, but crosses the plate 15 mph slower.

Stuff
Nasty, Flamethrower
Control Pitcher
Crafty

Having a 95 mph fastball does not mean a pitcher is more likely to get injured if he has been around the league for a while. Beware of young pitchers with "nasty" stuff. Kerry Wood burst onto the scene with a 98 mph fastball and the most wicked 92 mph curveball anyone had ever seen. His freakish arm generated so much torque, his curveball started at the hitter's head and ended with a swinging strike at a ball two feet off the plate. That great pitch had a horrible effect on his elbow causing him to miss the better part of two seasons. Now he throws a less strenuous version of the pitch and sticks mostly to fastballs.

Curt Schilling was plagued with injuries early in his career. Now, he is a workhorse, able to finish games and rack up the innings. He also is a model of efficiency, rare for a strikeout pitcher. He regularly is one of the league leaders in fewest bases on balls per inning pitched. Schilling will throw 90% to 95% fastballs during a game, minimizing the times his arm has to deal with arm wrenching breaking balls. He knows the strength of his game is his fastball and does not deviate from it. What makes Schilling so rare is that he is not just a power pitcher; he is also a control pitcher.

Most control pitchers are typically pitchers who throw between 88 mph and 92 mph. Their pinpoint control allows them to manipulate hitters into getting themselves out early in the count. Greg Maddux is the prototype control pitcher. He relies on his reputation for throwing strikes and the movement of his fastball to keep his pitch counts at a remarkably low level. In recent years, Maddux has run into injury troubles. In the eight years from 1988, when he established himself as a dominant pitcher, to his last Cy Young Award in 1995, Maddux averaged 100.4 pitches per game. In the past eight years since, he has averaged only 87.4 pitches per game and only 82.0 in the last three years. His pitching coach claims that the changing strike zone has hurt his ERA and BB totals in recent years. This is probably true since his pitches per inning have risen slightly. Fewer pitches per game yet more per inning means his innings are decreasing per start. That usually translates into fewer wins.

Older players often complain that by the time they finally figured out the game of baseball, their bodies stopped doing the things it was once capable of doing.

His problems have not been arm related ones, but leg and back injuries. This is another source of pitcher injuries. Maddux, unlike Schilling or Roger Clemens is not known for his off-season conditioning. In a recent interview, he said he never lifts weights. It may have worked for him in the past, but unless he changes his conditioning regimen, look for nagging injuries to hamper his performance in his final years in the league. Pitchers and hitters are continuing to put up terrific numbers at advanced ages these days. The most believable explanation for this is that advances in conditioning allow players to take advantage of their experience. Older players often complain that by the time they finally figured out the game of baseball, their bodies stop doing the things they were once capable of doing. Look for the pitchers who stay in top condition so they can perform at a high level all year long.

Crafty pitchers are ones who just seem to stay in games despite not having great stuff or especially good control. Names like John Burkett, Kirk Reuter, and even Tom Glavine come to mind. These pitchers are not high on your list of fantasy starters because they typically have high ratios and few strikeouts. Unlike control pitchers, they nibble on the corners and tend to have high pitch counts for the innings they pitch. High pitch counts usually mean a greater likelihood of injuries. Mediocre fantasy statistics plus a higher probability of injury means draft them at your own risk.

Specialists

Shifting from pitching to another category of player that merits special consideration, let us look at specialists. Fantasy players who dominate in a single category are a rare breed. Having one of these players can almost automatically vault your team into contention in that category. The categories where a player is most likely to dominate are Steals and Saves. The main reason for this is that there are few players in the league capable of making significant contributions in these categories. Those that are tend to contribute far more than the median player does. Baseball statisticians and Sabermetricians make the argument that the value of Steals and Saves in real baseball is overstated. If this is true, why do fantasy leagues continue to use these statistics? One reason may be that such statistics present an interesting challenge for the fantasy owner. Players who help your team the most in these categories typically do not contribute much in other categories. If they do, they are outrageously expensive.

Steals and Saves force fantasy owners to make tradeoffs. With leading home run hitters, Runs and RBIs closely correlate to HRs. It is rare to have a player be a great home run hitter and not be a leading run producer. Sluggers tend to be muscle-bound, lumbering giants such as Jim Thome, Jason Giambi, and Richie Sexson. Players excelling at stealing bases will probably score a decent amount of runs – mostly because of their spot in the batting order – but in most cases will not help much in HRs and RBIs. The best base stealers tend to be smaller, slim, and nimble. Ichiro, Luis Castillo, and Juan Pierre have physiques built for speed, not power. Closers, who help you in Saves, generally do not help much in Wins, Ks, ERA, and WHIP. While Closers may have excellent ERAs and WHIP ratios, their limited innings pitched contribute less to a team in these categories than starting pitchers or other relievers.

The challenge with drafting specialists is what you have to do with the rest of your team to find a place for them.

Run producers that also steal bases are very rare talents and usually command extremely high draft prices. The same goes for the elite closers who are so good that they make significant contributions in every category. There is little room for interpretation when valuing these players. Everyone knows their value to a team. Specialists are different though. For years, owners have wondered what to do with players such as Roger Cedeno and Jose Mesa. These players are far superior to the average player in one category, but inferior in most other categories. How much are they worth?

According to many fantasy magazines and other resources that assign dollar values to players, they can be quite valuable. If these players do perform as expected, they can certainly help your team. The challenge with drafting these players though is what you have to do with the rest of your team to find a place for them. If you are going to find a place for Juan Pierre on your team, you are going to have to get your HRs and RBIs elsewhere. No matter how many bases he steals, he will never be a great slugger. You can alter your draft strategy easily enough to accommodate such a player.

Players who specialize in steals and saves tend to fluctuate wildly in their performance.

There is a definite downside to altering your strategy around a single player. If that player does not perform as expected for whatever reason, your team may never recover from the loss. In the case of a steals specialist, during the draft you had to give up speed throughout the rest of your team so you could afford more HR and RBI producers to accommodate his lack of power. The rest of your team will have less speed than it otherwise would have had since you centered your draft strategy on one speedy player. You will likely end up with the minimum points in that one category, making it next to impossible to compete with more balanced teams. Your team's competitiveness will rest with a single player.

Player Unpredictability

There is more risk involved when pinning your hopes on a single player. Not only is the impact of that one player not performing as expected extremely costly, the likelihood of it happening is also quite high. Players who specialize in steals and saves tend to fluctuate wildly in their performance. Closers lose their jobs quicker than just about any position. If they blow a few saves, their managers are liable to go with another reliever. If closers fail, it affects the morale of the rest of the team. For this reason, Saves are quite unpredictable. Base stealers tend to fluctuate for other reasons. They may experience nagging leg injuries that may not be enough to sideline them, but are enough to reduce their steals drastically. Being traded to a team that runs very little can limit a player's attempts. If a stolen base threat is traded to the Oakland A's, who believe steals are overrated, you might want to pass on him. You might surmise the same about the New York Mets since Alomar and Cedeno both had sub-par stolen base performances in 2003. Art Howe, an Oakland A's transplant was the manager, but he only started managing in 2003. Bobby Valentine was the manager from 1996 through 2002. It was also under his tenure that Cedeno stole 66 bases in 1999 and 55 bases in 2001. How do you explain that? Stolen base production can suffer for a variety of reasons that are difficult to pinpoint. The following tables illustrate the great fluctuation in steals from year to year among some of the fastest players in the league.

Table 16: Steals for select leading base stealers

YEAR	CASTILLO	CEDENO	PIERRE	ALOMAR
1999	50	66	N/A	37
2000	62	25	7	39
2001	33	55	46	30
2002	48	25	47	16
2003	21	14	65	12

These numbers can be extremely frustrating when it comes to properly assigning a valuation to such players. Castillo and Cedeno produced feast or famine results between 1999 and 2003. If you drafted Castillo or Cedeno after each of their 60+ steal seasons, you clearly would have been disappointed. They undoubtedly were expensive players at the draft. Teams expected them to deliver 50-60 steals so they had little need to obtain more speed among the rest of their starters. These two probably destroyed the chances of thousands of fantasy league teams after their big years. Even more disturbing is that the same thing happened to both of them twice in only a five-year span.

Pierre and Alomar were equally unpredictable but in different ways. Pierre increased his steals nearly 40% in 2003. His owners must have been pleasantly surprised, but no valuation method could have possibly predicted such an increase. Alomar had stolen 30 or more bases three years in a row from 1999 to 2001. His nearly 50% drop in 2002 was cause for some alarm, but many owners chalked it up as a fluke and bid him up to prices reflecting the belief that he would reach the 30+ steals level once again.

Table 17: Games played for leading base stealers

YEAR	CASTILLO	CEDENO	PIERRE	ALOMAR
1999	128	155	N/A	159
2000	136	74	51	155
2001	134	131	156	157
2002	146	149	152	149
2003	152	148	162	140

With such inconsistency, you might conclude that serious injuries may have been the main culprit. Table 17 shows the amount of games each player played in during the same period. Throwing out Pierre's rookie season when he stole only seven bases and played in 51 games, the only significant drop in games occurred in 2000 with Cedeno. Serious injuries cannot explain the fluctuations of the other players, nor do they explain Cedeno's precipitous drop in steals in 2002 and 2003 when his number of games played actually increased over his 55-steal year in 2001.

Changing your draft strategy to accommodate a specialist carries tremendous risk. You incur the risk of having all your steals come from one player – putting all your eggs in one basket. The consequences of that player not performing as expected can be severe. Additionally, the players whose performance your entire team is counting on tend to be among the most unpredictable in the game. Drafting specialists and altering your team around them is a high-risk strategy - one that you might want to let your opponents employ.

Case Study

Juan Pierre – Great steals, no power. Sure, he will help you tremendously in steals, but you will suffer in HR and RBIs so much that you will have to spend a tremendous amount on power hitters to compensate.

Hitter	R	HR	RBI	SB	AVG
J. Pierre	100	1	41	65	0.305

You may be thinking, "The winner of my league in 2003 had Pierre on his team, and he was a big part of why he won." That may certainly be true. More likely, your opponent benefited, not because Pierre stole so much, but because he stole so many more bases than the rest of the league expected. Moving from Colorado, a great hitter's park, to Florida, a great pitcher's park, indicated to most owners that his other numbers – the ones that normally kill his owner's team – RBIs, HR, Runs, and Average would dip significantly. Additionally, his individual numbers had been trending down across the board. He was clearly someone to stay away from since his expected performance was minimal. Therefore, his draft value was much lower than it normally would have been. If everyone expected Pierre to steal 65 bases instead of his usual 45, they would have bid him up or someone would have drafted him earlier. The team with Pierre on it would have been weaker. Either it would have fewer dollars for the rest of its players, or the quality of each player drafted would be worse. File that under the luck category. That is going to happen. Sometimes it is in your favor, sometimes it is not.

The point is that there will be surprises for the better and for the worse. Pierre surprised for the better, but not because he is a specialist. He had a career year, as did his teammate Mike Lowell. You can probably name dozens of players who were significantly better than anyone would have expected – Carlos Delgado, Gary Sheffield, Carlos Lee, Javy Lopez, Edgar Renteria, etc. As a specialist, Pierre is still a risk. How many steals would you expect from him next year? 65 or 45. Some things are certain though. He will not help your team in at least a couple of categories. Actually, he will hurt your team. Remember from the valuation chapter that you have to compare him against the average replacement player. The comparison might look like this:

HITTER	R	HR	RBI	SB	AVG
J. Pierre	100	1	41	65	0.305
Avg. Player	87	23	85	11	0.290
Difference	**+13**	**-22**	**-44**	**+54**	**+0.015**

Looking at it from a perspective of category ranking points, here are Pierre's numbers:

HITTER	R	HR	RBI	SB	AVG
J. Pierre	0.7	-4.5	-2.3	10.7	1.0

It is obvious that Pierre can almost single-handedly win you steals, but you would have lost nearly seven spots in the standings in HR and RBI. This was a career year too. He was a top fantasy performer in 2003 and would certainly be drafted for a high price the next year. Just realize that if his steals do dip to his career averages, and the examples given indicate that it is a real possibility, Pierre is not far from being a below average player. In fact, if he stole about 40 bases – still six more than Ichiro stole in 2003, he would be just an average player.

Players with Unique Statistical Characteristics

After warning you about staying away from specialists who are great in one category, but tend to hurt you in others, a few players present a special value to your team. The following players are not just one-category wonders; they are great all-around players who can offer irreplaceable advantages in a few categories.

The point of this section is NOT to provide you with a comprehensive guide to players, but to point out the characteristics of great fantasy players. There are not many players available out there like the following. They will not come cheap. Let these player write-ups serve as an example of what to look for, and how to apply some of the valuation techniques previously discussed. Maybe you will discover the next Roy Halladay, or draft an underappreciated, but improving player.

Randy Johnson

If he is healthy, he should be the most valuable single player in the league. That is of course a big if since he is 40 years old and is coming off an injury that ruined his last season. When he is on his game though, he is as good as just about anyone in any starting pitching category, but he is especially great at strikeouts. If your league counts strikeouts, Johnson cannot be beat. He alone will account for about 35% of an average team's strikeouts. You can generally count on Roy Halladay and Bartolo Colon to be two of the better fantasy strikeout pitchers. Together, they struck out fewer players than Johnson did in his last full season, 2002.

Certainly, there will soon be a time when Johnson's age catches up to him. Who is a candidate to be the next Randy Johnson? Kerry Wood seems to have the potential. He is a dominant strikeout pitcher with the ability to put up superior numbers in every pitching category – except saves or course. Others might be Jason Schmidt, Josh Beckett, and Mark Prior.

Curt Schilling

Much like Johnson, Schilling is an outstanding all-around pitcher. Schilling has established himself as a top strikeout pitcher, but in recent years, he has challenged Johnson for the strikeout crown with 300+ Ks. Schilling also has an outstanding WHIP ratio because he challenges hitters with his outstanding stuff and control. He is also four years younger than Johnson is and will continue to share co-ace responsibility with Pedro in Boston.

The closest young pitcher to Schilling that comes to mind is Mark Prior with his excellent control and high strikeout totals. Others are Roy Halladay, Roy Oswalt, and Javier Vazquez.

Pedro Martinez

There was a time when no pitcher compared to Martinez for his all-around dominance. He was so much better than everyone else was; he drew comparisons with the all time best. Even though he continues to lead the league in ERA and ranks with the best in just about every category, he is not the same pitcher he once was. He has lost 5 mph on his fastball – not a good sign – and struggles to go past 7 innings in a game. He is great, but you have to factor in potential injuries when he comes up at your draft.

Other pitchers that have exhibited signs of deterioration are Greg Maddux, Tom Glavine, and Al Leiter.

Roy Halladay

2003 AL Cy Young winner Roy Halladay is a great pitcher to have on your fantasy team. His best quality is that he gives you innings, lots of them. He ranks among the leaders in complete games and innings pitched. Normally, you might be concerned by his number of innings pitched. Is it a coincidence that Johnson and Schilling missed significant portions of the 2003 season after each logging 260 innings the year before? Halladay threw 266 innings in 2003. He has had an unusual increase in innings pitched over the last few years going from 67 to 105 to 239 to 260. As scary as that looks, Halladay does have one thing going for him, his number of pitches per inning has dropped in each of those years as well. In fact, his 13.6 pitches per inning in 2003 were the lowest of any starting pitcher in the Major Leagues. He still throws a ton pitches in a season, but if he wears down, do not blame him, blame his manager.

Other young pitchers with very low pitches per innings pitched are Mark Mulder, Matt Morris, and Tim Hudson. Some others that have yet to emerge as top pitchers are Sydney Ponson, Miguel Batista, Brian Lawrence, Kyle Lohse, and Vincente Padilla.

Billy Wagner

Eric Gagne and John Smoltz get the headlines as far as closers go. Watching Gagne pitch is like watching a cartoon and Smoltz has had a storied career as a starter to cement his reputation as a dominant pitcher. They have been incredible, no doubt. Look at Wagner's numbers though, and he has posted seasons that rank with the best in history. It just so happens that Gagne and Smoltz are doing it at the same time. Gagne and Smoltz will go for the most in your league, but Wagner is nearly as good with much less fanfare.

Other quietly outstanding pitchers are Hideo Nomo, Troy Percival, Jorge Julio, Miguel Batista, and Kip Wells.

Barry Bonds

Barry Bonds is a 6-time MVP. He probably could have been an 8-time MVP if the voting was based solely on statistical dominance. There is no question that Bonds is the most feared hitter in the league. However, he may not be the most valuable fantasy league player. The reason is that pitchers simply do not pitch to him, so he cannot put up the traditional numbers that most fantasy leagues are based on. He will help you in HR and he will have a great BA, and score runs, but his RBIs will suffer for lack of opportunities. He can still steal a couple of bases now and then, but for him, that category is inconsequential. Do keep in mind that his BA will have less impact on your team than another player with the same BA since he will have fewer At Bats. If your league does not count measures such as, OBP, SLG, or OPS, Bonds will be a better player for his MLB team than he will be for yours.

Bonds is in a league of his own. There are few very high average hitters whose BA you should discount because of the amount of walks they receive. To a much lesser extent, Jorge Posada and Brian Giles fit the bill. Conversely, there are poor average hitters who are otherwise productive. Since they get fewer ABs, their poor BAs will hurt you less. Lance Berkman, Jim Thome, and Erubiel Durazo are examples.

Alfonso Soriano

Soriano is a rare talent with tremendous speed and power. He is also young and would seem to be one of the fantasy elite for years to come. Recently, he has come under fire for his lack of selectiveness at the plate. Since he rarely walks, he strikes out at an alarming rate. While Soriano puts up tremendous numbers as a leadoff hitter, his fantasy owners do not care about his OBP and hope his real life manager moves him to the third slot in the lineup. Keep abreast of developments with his MLB team that might alter his fantasy productivity.

Hank Blalock, Rocco Baldelli, Angel Berroa, Joe Crede, Carl Crawford and Shea Hillenbrand are all young players who have put up good numbers despite poor BB/SO ratios. These players are supremely talented, but if they struggle with the bat, keep an eye on them.

Vladimir Guerrero

A power and speed machine like Soriano, Vlad has actually learned how to harness his aggressiveness and become more selective at the plate. That combined with his amazing talent makes him a fantasy force of nature. If healthy, he could be the most productive fantasy player in baseball. He has had back problems, which are always troublesome for baseball players. Be aware that this might cut down on his power numbers and steal attempts. His speed is what suffered the most in 2003. While his HRs dipped from 39 to 25, his steals dropped from 40 to nine. If his steals are down again in 2004, expect his draft value to drop as well.

Other players who might be slowing down are Ichiro Suzuki and Bobby Abreu. Ichiro has relied on his speed so much. As he enters his 30s, do not be surprised if the downtrend in SBs is a precursor to fewer infield hits. With the dangerous yet selective Jim Thome batting behind him, what manager is going to give Abreu the green light to steal at will?

Alex Rodriguez

Alex Rodriguez is simply the best offensive fantasy player available. He not only puts up unparalleled offensive statistics, he is a Gold Glove shortstop. With some great offensive middle infielders and catchers, you have to worry about their teams moving them to other positions. His defensive prowess insures that he will continue to give his fantasy owners a tremendous positional advantage at shortstop. Rodriguez consistently produces outstanding numbers every year because he is also one of the most durable players in the Major Leagues.

Other top producers who are amazingly durable are Miguel Tejada, Richie Sexson, Carlos Delgado, Juan Pierre, and Jeff Bagwell.

Larry Walker

Larry Walker may not deserve to still be considered a superstar, but he always represented an interesting dilemma for fantasy owners. When healthy, he is a very productive player. For a number of years, you could argue that he was the most productive player per plate appearance in the Majors. The problem is, without fail, he would get hurt and miss several games per year. He was a tantalizing pick because if he could ever play 162 games, he would certainly have put up monster numbers. Many owners paid superstar prices for him only to be disappointed. Often injured players may not be as bad as they seem. If you know Larry Walker will hit 35 HR, hit .320 and drive in 110 runs in 120 games, he is still a monster. Add to that ¼ of the production of an average player since you will replace him with another player for the 40 games he is injured. You get about 40 HR, .310 BA, and 130 RBI. Not bad.

Other often-injured players who are top producers per game played are Juan Gonzalez, Jim Edmonds, Ellis Burks, Manny Ramirez, J.D. Drew, and Ken Griffey Jr.

Established superstars can be very important to your fantasy team, but they will not come cheap. Some of the characteristics to look for when you are trying to find the next wave of superstars are:

Pitchers
- Solid overall numbers, but dominant in one category such as saves or strikeouts
- Excellent control, but high strikeout totals
- Minimal signs of deterioration
- Low number of pitches per inning
- Quietly outstanding, but overshadowed by others

Special Considerations

Hitters
- Look at total Hits and AB, not just BA
- No reasons for them to stop stealing
- Solid contributors who are also durable
- Solid BB/SO ratio
- Very productive per plate appearance

Look for these characteristics in players that you draft, and you can set up your team for some pleasant surprises. You may just discover the next superstar.

How can you reduce the risk of injuries to your pitchers?

What position does your league under appreciate the most?

Which players will emerge as the next great ones?

Chapter 6. Management Style

Every manager has a particular management style. It is important for competitive reasons to know your opponents and their styles so you can anticipate their strategies. It is equally important, if not more important to understand your own style. You cannot have a comprehensive strategy without considering your own management style. If you do not know what kind of manager you are, how will you put together a team that matches what you want to accomplish?

One obvious common mistake that fantasy owners make is that they rarely draft teams to support their management style. They may know what they want to do, but they do not have the team to support those efforts. To illustrate this point, it might be helpful to identify a couple of common management styles.

Buy and Hold

This style is the patient owner's approach. The philosophy is that over time, players will generally perform the way you expected them to perform. This of course is in the context of a team. Some players will over perform and others will under perform, but overall your team will do as expected. The belief here is that you just do not know which player will do what and when. You may think that a player who has done exceptionally well in the first half of the season is due for a collapse. A more active owner might try to pull the trigger on a trade. The problem is that same player might just go on to have a career year. You just never know with individual players, but with your team, you have a good idea.

Of course, you might not make many moves simply because you do not like to, or you are too busy. Those are legitimate reasons that you should take into consideration. It may be too much work for you to keep up with all the available free agents, or you just do not want to invest the time it takes to structure a deal. Working out trades can be complicated and time consuming.

An advantage the Buy and Hold owner has is that he does not risk over-managing. If you are the kind of person that agonizes over the player you traded away that ended up doing well, this might be the style for you. In leagues where you incur fees for transactions during the year, this type of owner faces a better risk-reward ratio.

Active Manager

On the other end of the spectrum, is the active manager. The active manager believes he can gain some sort of edge by making multiple transactions. He might trade for a player who appears to be having a breakout year. At the same time, he might trade for another player who historically has performed better than he has so far in the current season. This type of owner puts faith in his intuition and ability to manage his team.

An advantage of being an active manager is that you theoretically can get a better feel for your league. By talking to other owners about potential trades, you open up a dialogue that can be the source of important intelligence. You might learn which players of yours others like. At the same time you can learn about the ones for which they care very little. A trade may not happen after the first conversation, but it might happen later when you really need it.

You should try to determine how involved you are going to be in:

- Establishing and Enforcing League Rules
- League Administration
- Valuation
- Strategy Creation
- Pre-Draft Preparation
- Trading Activity
- Free Agent Pickups
- Roster Changes

All of these activities will require your time and commitment. Do you know how much you are willing to give? If you are not willing to commit your time, what resources can you turn to for help to execute your strategy as you envision it?

Season Management

Generally, how you manage your team will depend on the rules of your league. Some leagues require a greater level of diligence than others do if you want to compete. Leagues where you can change your lineup on a daily basis can be very demanding. Often, the winner of such a league is the one who has the most time or the greatest discipline. If you do participate in a league that needs your daily attention, you must be diligent or you are sure to do poorly. That is the minimum level. Unless there are game limits, you cannot compete with an owner who moves players in and out of his lineup each day to maximize games

You simply have to be able to commit enough time so you can execute your strategy optimally.

played unless you are willing to do the same. He will have one or two more games played per position than you will after a week. Over the course of the season, it could be hundreds.

Even if your league requires only weekly interaction, there will be some owners who actively look for free agents and routinely alter their lineups. You simply have to be able to commit enough time so you can execute your strategy optimally. If you cannot commit the time, you should change leagues, or you need to alter your strategy to work with the amount of time you can commit.

Maximizing Starts

A common practice for managing your pitching staff is maximizing starts for Wins - and Strikeouts in 5x5 leagues. It is so common that it could hardly be called a strategy, but it is at least worth mentioning. For weekly leagues, owners try to put in starting pitchers who will get two starts. Most pitchers will have only one start per week. Owners in a league that sets lineups by Sunday night look to start pitchers who will go on the Monday or Tuesday of the following week. In most cases, those pitchers will pitch again on Saturday or Sunday. This should be standard procedure unless the match-ups dictate differently. You might prefer one start from an excellent pitcher to two by a mediocre one. If one out of a pitcher's two starts is in a hitter's park like Colorado where he is likely to pitch poorly, you may not want to play him. Pitching against good teams or against a top starter may be reasons not to pitch a player with two starts. All things being equal though, go with pitchers who will get two starts.

You can support your season management style with your draft. If you do not like to try to maximize starts, you may consider drafting a team that has superstar starters. You know that they will be in your lineup every week. It will make your decision making process much simpler. If you only have a few open starting pitching slots remaining, you can maximize starts there. With enough pitchers, you might be able to get two starts in those slots every week. If you do not mind changing your lineup, you could draft a team with few superstars. Instead, you could get many interchangeable, solid starters. That way, you simply play whichever players get two starts in any given week.

Support Your Style with Strategy

In the next chapter, you will look at drafting strategies. Before you read that section, you had better determine your style so you can identify the drafting strategies that will support it. Here is an example of how my style fits my strategy:

My style is that of an active trader. There are certain strategies that work better with my style than they would if I were less active. For instance, I often use the hoarding strategy to try to influence the draft dynamics. I may leave the draft with far too many expensive players at one position than I could possibly fit into my starting lineup. If I am going to implement this strategy, I know that for me to optimize my team's potential, it is imperative that I trade. A laid-back style will not suffice. I may have to make multiple trades involving multiple partners to shape my team the way I originally envisioned it would look like.

One year in my league, my team was exceptionally strong in pitching and another team was exceptionally strong in hitting. I had built up a large lead in most of the pitching categories a third of the way into the season. The two of us ended up trading a ton of pitching for a ton of hitting. A person with a Buy and Hold style might think we overdid it. My trading partner received Curt Schilling and Pedro Martinez in exchange for Vladimir Guerrero and Shawn Green. He built up a sizeable lead in pitching, far surpassing my team by the time the trading deadline rolled around. I had since traded away some of the hitting I received to bolster my pitching again. My original trading partner though, failed to trade away his pitching for hitting help and ended up dominating pitching while pulling up the rear in all of the hitting categories. I won the league, and he ended up in the middle of the pack.

My trading partner just did not optimize his team's value because he did not follow through on the advantages he had.

I still contend that our original trade was very fair in terms of talent and raw statistical value. My trading partner just did not optimize that value because he did not follow through on the advantages he had. I believe our two teams would have fought it out for the title that year. It was a case of an excellent trade for both sides. It was also a case of his management style failing to support a strategic decision.

Management Style

What is your management style?

What are the management styles of the other owners in your league?

Chapter 7. The Draft

How you draft should reflect and compliment your management strategy. If you do not plan to be an active trader, you should draft a "complete" team, solid at every position. If you are an active trader, you should consider drafting for value disregarding position to a certain extent, knowing that you will have more leverage for a trade after the draft.

Draft Type

There are two predominant types of fantasy league drafts – the *straight draft*, and the *auction*. This book will focus more on the auction type of draft, because it is more complicated, and the strategies need to be a bit more sophisticated.

If your league does a straight draft, there is less gamesmanship to worry about. Teams can draft any player remaining when their turn comes around. For this reason, there are very few surprises. Most owners will prepare a ranked list of players. They will probably start with the best available player and then go for positions as they fill spots. You might find that your well laid out strategies take a back seat to improvisation when players you think should have gone earlier are still available. You cannot disguise your hand because if you do not pick the best player available, someone else will.

You cannot disguise your hand because if you do not pick the best player available, someone else will.

Serious fantasy baseball leagues tend to prefer the auction style because of the gamesmanship involved. In an auction, you pick a player for everyone in the league to bid on. Just because you put a player up for auction, it does not mean you will get him. In fact, you probably do not want to end up with a player you bring up unless it is very late in the draft. A basic auction tactic is to bring up players you do not need or want so the ones you want will come up later when your opponents have less money to spend on them.

Going on about how to set up your league for one draft type or another would probably bore you to tears. You probably already know the rules or your league commissioner can explain them to you in a matter of minutes. It really is straightforward. In general, drafting for value means drafting a player who you think should have gone higher based on his expected performance. That statement is true whether your league does a straight draft or an auction. The rest of this book will assume your league uses an auction. The term "draft" will be used generically to refer to the process of initially selecting your players. If it uses a straight draft, you should easily be able to see how it applies to you.

Draft Day Dynamics

Draft day in most leagues is probably the single best day of the baseball season for fantasy owners. Many leagues have participants who hail from all around the country. Your entire league may only be in the same room once all year - and this is it. If your league is anything like mine, it will feel like one big reunion party. Even in online leagues, everyone feels a palpable energy at the draft.

Along with that energy comes distractions. There is usually a good dose of playful banter and maybe just a tad of drinking going on. It is easy to lose focus on drafting at your best. New players should take note of this and do a little extra planning ahead of time.

You can learn quite a bit about your competition if you can look past the distractions and see the signs. During the bidding for any given player, there is usually a bit of gamesmanship going on, but owners also give off legitimate signals. One example of a bidding dialogue for a player such as Barry Bonds might go something like this:

Owner 1: $30!
Owner 2: $35
Owner 3: $36
Owner 2: $37
(Pause in the action)
Moderator: Going once, going twice…
Owner 3: $38
Owner 2: $39
(Pause in the action)
Moderator: Going once, going twice…
Owner 3: Hold on man! (As he flips through a magazine to check the projections again.)
Everyone: (Chiming in) Come on! This is going to take forever. Hurry up! He's worth $50. You love Bonds.
Owner 3: Okay, okay, $42!
Owner 2: $43
Owner 3: $44
Owner 2: Take him!
Owner 3: Shoot. I should have stopped at $39.

Observe how peer pressure affects individuals. Do they get carried away with their bidding? There will usually be several lulls in the action, with owners feigning as if they are close to their limits. Look to see

Fantasy Baseball Strategy

when owners pause to recheck the stats or when they tell the others to "shut up". That usually means they are about to go past their previously determined dollar amount. You can get a fairly accurate read on certain owners if you are observant. That can be useful information later in the draft.

Top fantasy players tend to be brought up for auction early in the draft. This is because competitively, you want your opponents to have as little money as possible when a player you want is up for bid. If for instance, you know that Rafael Palmiero will go for about $30, but you already have a solid first baseman, putting him out for bid and letting someone else get him means another team with $30 less money to spend. Few top players slip past the beginning rounds. If some do, you can be sure that everyone knows it and several owners are saving their money for those players.

Just do not let your opponents get the best of you because you let the environment influence your decision-making.

As the draft reaches the later stages and owners have crossed off the top players from their lists, they search for prospects and bench players. Owners are predictably going to spend less time preparing for the 279th best player than they would the 10th best. When the name of a relatively unheard of prospect comes up, owners scramble for their magazines to read up on the reports. Sometimes, you can bring up a prospect for bid early and throw people off. When people are preoccupied with deciding between drafting players such as Garciaparra or Soriano, they may not want to bother figuring out how a minor leaguer fits into their budgets. You might be able to sneak one by the league and draft him yourself, or force someone to pay $7 for a player who would normally go for $2 at the end of the draft.

There are all sorts of little tricks and games people play. If you have participated in live auctions before, they will not surprise you. Even if you know all the tricks though, it is still easy to get carried away with all the excitement and distraction of the day. If you can use the energy to your advantage, that is great. Just do not let your opponents get the best of you because you let the environment influence your decision-making. Have fun on draft day, but try to keep focused on the reason you are there - to draft the best team.

Organization

It is a tremendous help to keep track of not only your team, but also everyone else's team. On one sheet of paper, or one computer spreadsheet, you can have access to valuable information about your opponents and their needs. This is an absolute must. This one sheet will give you information on relative strengths and weaknesses of every team at a given point in the draft. It will be your early warning system for identifying your opponents' strategies. You will also know the teams that seem to be putting together your main competition.

This one sheet will give you information on relative strengths and weaknesses of every team at a given point in the draft.

Be prepared for the later rounds. There are rarely bargains available in the early rounds. Players such as Vladimir Guerrero will go for a lot of money. There is no mystery there. The difference between a strong draft and a weak one is usually determined by what happens at the end of it. Everyone is tired, and most people are simply trying to fill positions, going down the list of a magazine to come up with a name. Every so often, a name of a retired, injured, or player not yet in the Major Leagues will come up. It is just a sign that the room is ripe for the picking. Here you can pick up valuable prospects and potential keepers for the next year at bargain basement prices. It is also a time when previously injured players who have fallen off the radar screens of most tend to pop up. By the time you throw the player out for auction, very few people have the buying power left over to do anything but agonize over the oversight. You have to manage your money and strike at a time that limits your opponents' ability to steal that player away from you.

Drafting for Depth

One of the first questions you have to ask yourself when preparing for the draft is what kind of depth you need, and where you need to draft. The main factor in determining the kind of depth you need is injuries, but there is more to a good depth strategy than consideration for injuries. Depth can affect your strategy in many ways:

- Overall attitude toward risk
- Position scarcity
- Type of players drafted
- Insurance against injury
- Insurance against loss of playing time
- Allowing for surprises

Going into the draft, you will have to gauge your overall attitude towards injury risk. This translates into whether you try to optimize your starting players, hoping the injury bug passes by your team, or give up a little starting talent to have reserves that are more competent. One consideration is the kind of overall talent your league has available. Some leagues draft from the entire Major Leagues. Others select from either the National or American League, while some draw from only a few teams. The larger your overall pool of talent, the more depth you will be able to draft. There will also be more free agents available after the draft. Trying to optimize your starters generally means you are willing to accept that you will not be able to replace a productive player with a comparable player. If you decide to take this route, your team production will likely be up and down. If you draft competent reserves, your team productivity will be more consistent throughout the season.

Depth and Trading Ability

There are two schools of thought when it comes to depth and your ability to make trades during the season. Some believe that it is difficult to dislodge a star player from an opponent without a star player in return. This would make a starter-optimized team better equipped to trade. It has an abundance of stars, complimented by relatively inferior players. The other school of thought is that teams with more depth have more players who are desirable to other teams, and thus have more trade possibilities. The truth is probably a combination of both. If you have a starter-optimized team, you will probably make fewer trades, but the ones you make will tend to be big, impact trades. A deep

Allowing for Surprises

You can do everything correctly, but without a little luck, you still will probably not win your league. Tilt the odds in your favor a bit by allowing yourself to be lucky. You can do this by speculating on players with upside potential. Having players on your team who are experiencing breakout seasons or career years can be a tremendous boost to your chances of winning. You might allocate a few extra spots on your roster for young phenoms who have yet to establish themselves in the league as stars. It might also be wise to take a flyer on players who have shown a high capacity in the past but have disappointed in recent years. Players such as Carlos Delgado and Richard Hidalgo had monster years followed by extremely disappointing ones. They could still prove to have another huge season left in them. You need to give your team a chance to get lucky. Drafting the reliable Jamie Moyer and hoping he leads the league in strikeouts is nothing but a pipe dream. Drafting fireball throwing A.J. Burnett and hoping he bounces back from injury gives you a chance to be surprised for the better. There is more to allowing for surprises than drafting. The Free Agency chapter will cover this subject in more detail.

> *You can do everything correctly, but without a little luck, you still will probably not win your league. Tilt the odds in your favor a bit by allowing yourself to be lucky.*

Depth to Support Your Strategy

Preparing for the draft, you will try to envision how your team will fall into place. You may know what positions you want to fill with star players. For instance, if you decide that you must have Ivan Rodriguez at catcher, you have a good idea that you will not need to spend much on a backup for him. Rodriguez will play in the majority of the games. You are not going to waste your money on a backup because unless you also draft Javy Lopez or Mike Piazza, players good enough to play at DH, no backup catcher is going to play for you unless Rodriguez gets hurt. Let's face it, if Rodriguez gets hurt, your team will suffer. The difference between the 15th best catcher in the league and any old catcher you can pick up as a free agent is virtually non-existent. Either one of them will produce only a fraction of what Rodriguez would have produced. Having spent $25 for Rodriguez, you might be apt to settle for a $1 or $2 backup, if you choose to keep one on your roster at all. The alternate strategy might be to draft an $8 catcher and a $6 backup. If you plan what you want to do at each position, you will know the kind of depth you will need to draft.

You start with an idea of how you would like your team to look. Then you put together the core areas around which you want to build your team.

This method of determining your team's depth is like putting your strategy together piece by piece. You start with an idea of how you would like your team to look. Then you put together the core areas around which you want to build your team. You may decide you want to draft a top catcher, a top shortstop, and one of the top three closers. This is the core part of your draft strategy. You do not overreach because you know that you have to remain flexible in case something unexpected occurs. Next, you work on the areas you would like to have a certain way. You are in control, so you can make these things happen if you choose. Here you would like to draft two-second tier starting pitchers – Tim Hudson and Roy Oswalt will do just fine. You would also like to add a power hitting first baseman. You are not sure if you will be able to afford all that, but you are willing to substitute an outfielder for the first baseman and three lesser pitchers will do if need be. After that, you hope you get certain players, but if there is too much demand for the players you like, you will have to move on.

Figure 3: Depth probability

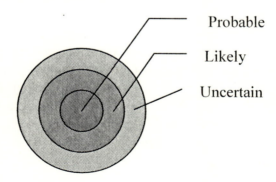

Build around your core strategy and become more and more flexible as you fill in the pieces. Your bench players fall into the outer, uncertain area. You do not have too much control over which bench players you will end up with unless you specifically set aside money for the players you want. What you do have control of is how much you will plan to spend on bench players for each position.

Risk Insurance

Having a strong bench can act as insurance against injuries. Your team is going to have injuries during the season. If you have many injuries, a strategy to draft a deep team will benefit you. If you have fewer injuries than expected, you may end up wasting some of your draft money. You could have paid less for a few bench players and upgraded one or two starting players for better ones. Having a deep team does not necessarily mean you will end up wasting your draft money. If you can turn around and trade some of that depth late in the year after you have weathered most of the injury storm, you may be able to optimize your team's potential.

This illustrates an interesting tradeoff. Draft for depth and you protect your team against injuries. You also have the ability to trade with another team that has run into injury problems itself. This puts you in a position of strength as a trader. Draft to optimize your starters from the beginning of the season, and injuries could put you in a trading position of weakness. You may have to trade away more of your stars – in addition to those you lost to injuries – to fill all of your holes. The tradeoff is

The tradeoff is whether you would rather be strong early or strong late in the year.

whether you would rather be strong early or strong late in the year.

The other type of insurance depth gives you is against the loss of playing time. Having a weak bench also exposes you to the fickleness of MLB managers. If they decide they would like to platoon your player, you may end up with not only poor replacement statistics for your injured starter, but a fraction of the at bats. A deep bench means fewer of your players will face such humbling assignments by their managers.

Hoarding

One draft strategy you can use is hoarding. Try to identify a specific position that (1) has relatively few quality players available and (2) tends to be overlooked or undervalued. An example of this strategy is illustrated in Chapter 3: Competitive Strategy using shortstops. Although you can use this method effectively at any position, the obvious positions where you can make an immediate impact are at shortstop and catcher. Most people consider these defensive positions in baseball. Any offensive production is a bonus. Each year, there will be exceptions to the rule. Recently, it has seemed that there has been a dearth of productive players at second base and third base. Positions where there are a few great players and then a severe drop-off in productivity are ripe for hoarding.

Price Adjustments

In the competitive strategy section, you learned that you could create value for yourself by putting the pressure on your opponents to react. The hoarding example used in that section also illustrated how owners acting in the best interests of their teams will try to trade with you. One overlooked benefit of hoarding, but possibly even more influential on the rest of the league is what the strategy does to subsequent prices.

If you are hoarding the top shortstops, the price of the remaining shortstops will increase substantially. Opponents will realize that there are fewer quality players at that position with everyone competing for them, including you. Some owners coming into the draft set on acquiring one of the top shortstops will go overboard trying to make their strategy fit the circumstances. On occasion, you will observe irrational exuberance as the prices skyrocket beyond all anticipation. This does not always happen, but even the most disciplined drafters can get carried away with their emotions. Even if they are able to acknowledge to themselves that they are bidding too much, they do not want to be held hostage to your trade demands after the draft. Little do they know that their attempts to avoid being held hostage falls right into your master plan. As they bid up the price of the next best player, the prices of the remaining players increase.

It becomes apparent that someone will be left out in the cold when the bidding is complete.

Such a strategy can surprise your opponents and make them react irrationally. Obviously, that is to your advantage, but their overbidding may in fact be rational from their perspectives. If they realize that they will be at a significant trading disadvantage after the draft, it may well make sense to spend an extra dollar or two on a player that will save them the trouble and cost later in the season. It is a conscious tradeoff. People avoid pain

Fantasy Baseball Strategy

and hassle. Bidding an extra fantasy dollar is easy to do.

Table 18: Price adjustment after hoarding

	SHORTSTOPS	EXPECTED PRICE	ACTUAL PRICE
1	*Alex Rodriguez**	*$42**	*$42**
2	*Miguel Tejada**	*$34**	*$32**
3	Nomar Garciaparra	$32	$37
4	Derek Jeter	$26	$29
5	Edgar Renteria	$20	$22
6	Orlando Cabrara	$18	$20
7	Angel Berroa	$17	$19
8	Rafael Furcal	$16	$18
9	Alex Cintron	$7	$8
10	Jimmy Rollins	$6	$7
11	Rich Aurilia	$4	$4
12	Christian Guzman	$3	$3
	League	$225	$240

Table 18 illustrates how the hoarding strategy might affect the prices of the remaining starting shortstops. In this example, you draft Alex Rodriguez and Miguel Tejada. You might even decide to draft Garciaparra or Jeter as well, but for simplicity sake, suppose it is just the two. You are able to draft Rodriguez for the expected price of $42 - nothing unusual here. You are a late bidder for Tejada and you act a bit nervous as if you do not want to be stuck with another shortstop. You mention that if ARod went for $42, Tejada is worth at least $35. The comments start flying across the room with laughter, "Stick him with Tejada! Yeah, what's he going to do with two shortstops?" You end up with Tejada for $32, $2 less than you originally projected he would go for in a normal auction. Your plan is working to perfection, all while your opponents are razzing you about how they stuck you!

The tables turn when you throw out for bid the next best shortstop available, Nomar Garciaparra. Throwing out players for auction who play a position that you have already filled is a predictable and common draft tactic. You start the bidding aggressively. If you end up with Garciaparra, that is fine. However, you would prefer to conserve your capital at this point. You have just signaled to the entire league that you are trying to monopolize the shortstops. The other owners pile in not wanting to be stuck with the dregs. You stuck them! You adroitly bow out of the bidding as the price surges past your projection to $37. You throw in a little zinger, "Nomar's going to be huge this year. I wish I could get him but I already have all the shortstops I can afford." After the price frenzy for Garciaparra, things settle down a bit, though you suspected they would have gotten out of hand had Derek Jeter put up his normal injury free numbers. Let us just suppose the rest of the shortstops go for about 10% more than expected on average because it becomes apparent that someone will be left out in the cold when the bidding is complete. There is usually less price impact on the less expensive players after most owners have secured their starters. The table reflects that. You masterfully made the other owners play a game of musical chairs for shortstops.

The league has just spent $240 on the first 12 shortstops drafted. Assuming the projections are reasonably accurate, the league overbid by $15. That does not tell the entire story though. More accurately,

Fantasy Baseball Strategy 141

the rest of the league paid a $17 premium while you picked up the two best shortstops in the game at a $2 discount.

Table 19: Price adjustment

Shortstops	Expected Price	Actual Price	Price Adjustment
Your Average Price	$38.00	$37.00	97%
Average Opponent Price	$14.90	$16.57	111%

While your shortstops cost you 3% less than expected, your opponents ended up paying 11% more for the same statistics out of their shortstop position they thought they would get. They also have less money to spend on other positions while you have an extra $2. You end up netting a 14% advantage over your opponents on the price of shortstops. You still have all the other positions to go. A couple of fantasy bucks here, a couple of fantasy bucks there, and all of a sudden, your opponents cannot execute their plans *You probably do not believe that you have the ability to evaluate players 14% better than your opponents can.* because they do not have enough money. You win again! All that other stuff about how hoarding increases your trading leverage during the season is just gravy at this point.

This is an example of why competitive strategy is so important. You probably do not believe that you have the ability to evaluate players 14% better than your opponents can. It is doubtful that your competitors are that much better than you are either. We all could be wildly wrong when it comes to optimally valuing players. No one had any idea that Bill Mueller was going to be the 2003 AL batting champion or that Esteban Loaiza would contend for the AL Cy Young Award. You probably should not be in a league with anyone able to predict those performances. That person probably has supernatural powers, and may be hazardous to your health. What you should know however, is that when you consciously force your opponents to pay more than they expected or to do something they had not planned on doing, you gain. That should be good enough.

Piling On

One year, a fellow hoarder greatly aided my strategic efforts. It was an unexpected surprise, but one that was greatly appreciated. I had long before realized that my league had traditionally under appreciated and thus undervalued starting pitching at my league's draft. In this respect, my league was quite common. My strategy was to overload my team with top-flight starting pitchers. In particular, I wanted primarily strikeout pitchers since my league counts strikeouts. We run a keeper league, so going into the draft, I already had John Smoltz, who Atlanta had tabbed to be its new closer that year. Another owner in my league, Kevin, would start the draft with Mark Mulder and Matt Morris whom he had drafted the year before at bargain basement prices. My first player drafted was Kerry Wood for $23, quickly followed by a bit of a stretch for Josh Beckett at $20. Then I drafted Pedro Martinez at $51 and everyone thought my pitching staff was complete. After Randy Johnson was drafted for $52,

Fantasy Baseball Strategy 143

Kevin, probably seeing that his pitching no longer was the best then drafted Mike Mussina for $35 and Barry Zito for $26. I looked around and I could see the other owners crossing off the top pitchers from their lists. When I ended up with Curt Schilling at $37, the room was in full fledge crisis mode. There were no more sure bet, stud pitchers left to draft.

I tried to throw out the next best starting pitcher for auction each time I had the opportunity, but one or two pitchers every 12 players hardly constituted a run. I must admit the draft did not progress exactly how I envisioned it. I felt a little left out in the cold as one top offensive player after another came up for bid, but having spent so much on pitching early, I was unable to participate. Things seemed grim, but then a funny thing happened. Finally, someone must have felt it was about time to pick up his first pitcher. The competitive bidding started up again. Pitchers that would have normally gone for $10 or less were going for $17 to $20. Owners were not just paying a few dollars more for their pitchers, they were paying 50%, 75%, even 100% more than expected. They put off the pain until the later rounds, but they had to pay the piper eventually. Another strange thing happened. It was as if the group had collectively decided that if there were not going to be any quality starters remaining, at least they were each going to get a top closer or two. This was fine with me since I already had John Smoltz who I rated as one of the top three closers in the Majors. Seven closers went for $25 or more, which was unheard of in my league. People were definitely off their game plans.

So how well did I do when held to the standard of the Fundamental Theorem of Fantasy Sports? I planned my strategy, and for the most part, things went as expected. I was a little worried for a while, but I was patient and things turned out even better than expected. I managed the same as if I knew the others' strategies. In fact, I knew their strategies, because I helped force them into it – so I gained.

How did my opponents do? Clearly, they managed differently than they had planned. If they had known my strategy was to draft all the top pitchers, they would have bid them up more to make my strategy more costly, or stayed in until they eventually got a few pitchers. They managed much differently than they would have had they known my strategy, so they lost.

Table 20: Fundamental Theorem of Fantasy Sports

If all strategies were known	**You**	
	Manage the Same	**Manage Differently**
Opponents – Manage the Same	You Benefit + Opponents Benefit = No Clear Advantage	You Lose + Opponents Benefit = Advantage Opponents
Opponents – Manage Differently	You Benefit + Opponents Lose = **Advantage You**	You Lose + Opponents Lose = No Clear Advantage

Predictability

Do not overlook an important aspect of drafting - predictability. Your goal should not always be to beat your opponent or get great bargains. If you can, that is great, but it is not always possible, nor necessary. Sometimes it is enough to have a solid plan work out as you expected it to. Predictability is about actually getting the output from a player, or your team that you originally expected.

Every league has at least one owner known for always betting on the come, or speculating on young players. He has the honor of having "found" Ichiro, Kerry Wood, and Josh Beckett. He scours the minor leagues for the top prospects hoping to get the next phenom before he becomes too expensive. It is important to identify up and coming players, but you have to factor in that their performances are largely unpredictable. In fact, most phenoms who eventually turn out to be great players struggle for at least a year or two. It is okay to *Injuries are the bugaboo of many fantasy league owners.* take a few risks, but you have to treat your team like an investment portfolio. With risk comes reward. You want the possibility of paying $5 and getting a $25 performance in return, but you have to be able to afford wasting that $5 if your bet does not pan out. You should balance those high-risk, high-reward investments with ones that are more predictable. Knowing that a good portion of your team is going to do what you expect of it has tremendous value.

Back in his heyday, Cal Ripken was a regular on my fantasy team. Other owners joked that I loved Ripken. Love might be a little over the top, but I certainly appreciated him as a fantasy player. There was nothing more predictable than Cal Ripken. You knew he was going to play every game, hit 20+ homers and drive in 90+ RBI. You also knew that he had a mediocre average and never stole bases. The best thing he did was free up a roster spot, and save at least $1 that otherwise would have had to have been spent on a backup shortstop. That kind of predictability - 2,153 games in a row - is unique. For that, he was worth paying the premium that came with people thinking I "loved" him. I had to make up for his shortcomings at other positions, but it was something that was easy to manage.

Injuries are the bugaboo of many fantasy league owners. For the most part, players who have avoided injuries will tend to avoid them in the future. Players that always seem to be hurt, tend to get hurt again. Sometimes you just cannot tell. You have to be leery when you see a player's bio that says he was one of only two major leaguers to play in all 162 games last year. You cannot be sure if that is a good thing, or a bad thing. He certainly was tough last season and has the ability to play through pain, but will that stubbornness come back to haunt him next season? All that wear and tear cannot possibly be good for his longevity. Playing so many games may start to affect his performance this year. Drafting to avoid injuries is a perplexing problem. What you can do is to try to avoid drafting too many players who have a history of being injury-prone.

Position Scarcity

You need to keep in mind that some positions are deeper than others are. At certain positions, after the top few players, there is a precipitous drop off in

Fantasy Baseball Strategy

performance. This should factor into your draft strategy. What is the worst player you are willing to accept at any one position? Would you rather have the top third baseman and the twentieth best outfielder, or the fifth best outfielder and the eighth best third baseman? These are tough decisions, but ones that you will have to make. In any draft, especially an auction, the player you draft in the second round may very well preclude you from drafting another player you want in the tenth round.

One method for determining depth at each position is to rank players by level. It is probably best to do this simple exercise after you have completed your valuation process. Rank your players by dollar value or point value. Then draw a line after the last acceptable player you are willing to draft at each position. No matter how the draft plays out, you do not want to be stuck with a player below the line. Now that you have identified the subset of players you will choose from, divide each player position into tiers. For each position, you might make about three tiers. Usually, it is obvious where there is a drop-off in talent level for each position. Those are your natural tier levels. Your tiers may resemble *Figure 3: Depth probability* from earlier in the chapter. Each position has a few players around which any owner could build his team. Then there are complimentary players and finally fill-in players. You can use different colors on your list for each level so you can compare position to position. You may have only three

The player you draft in the second round may very well preclude you from drafting another player you want in the tenth round.

shortstops in your top level, but there are eight outfielders who you feel are at that same level. This is a good way to set goals for your team. You can go into the draft with a plan to select two top-level infielders, three second-tier infielders, three third-tier outfielders, four second-tier starting pitchers, and two fourth-tier relievers. This method makes it easy to pass on players as long as there is still a player remaining in the same tier level at that position.

This tier method is useful with or without in-depth valuation analysis as described in Chapter 4. The valuation process can help you uncover the players who can contribute to your team, but do not have the name recognition. If you are surprised to see a name on your list, your competition will probably be surprised as well. If you decide that you are still going to buy a magazine in addition to your own valuation, pick one that is popular with your opponents so you can compare your league specific list with the list the most owners in your league will be using. If there are some undiscovered gems, you can be confident that your opponents will not value them as much as you do.

Another factor related to position scarcity is how easily you will be able to trade for a competent player in each position.

Another factor related to position scarcity is how easily you will be able to trade for a competent player in each position. Players with positions of great scarcity tend to be difficult to trade, simply because it is difficult to fill the gap left by that player. People do not like to make a trade that leaves them with a gaping hole in their lineup. It stymies trade talks. Only the most willing and the most creative are able to break the impasse. If you think you are going to want to have a top catcher on your team, you had better draft one, because trading for one will be difficult.

Drafting for Scarcity

One strategy centers your draft on players that provide your team superiority in positions that have few productive players. Be aware, that just about every owner in your league will institute some form of this strategy in one way or another. Most owners will be aware of the positions that are going to be hard to fill. Your core strategy could be to make sure you are strong in these areas of scarcity. The distinction is that you center your draft on getting some of the best players in these positions versus not being stuck with a lousy one. You will not let anyone deter you from your goal, while others may if something unexpected drives up the price of these players. That unexpected force is of course: You.

Be aware, that just about every owner in your league will institute some form of this strategy in one way or another.

Traditionally, the infield positions other than first base have been weak offensively. Back in the early 1990s, the team that drafted Mike Piazza had an incredible positional advantage at catcher. No catchers even approached his production. The thinking here was that you might have to accept lesser players in deeper positions, usually outfield, but your advantage at catcher would more than make up for the difference. The marginal difference between an elite outfielder and a second-tier one in HRs may have been 5-10. The difference between Piazza and the next best catcher was about 25 HRs. The strategy to pick up Piazza was a solid one in concept, but everyone was aware of the advantage he presented, so they always bid him up accordingly.

Things have changed. There is no longer a single dominant player like Piazza. Even if there was, top outfielders now hit 40+ HRs. The marginal value above the average second tier outfielder has increased. Other traditionally weak positions have become much stronger. Shortstop has historically been a defense-first position, but for fantasy owners, the new breed of bigger, offensive-minded shortstops has given them many more alternatives. These changes can be used to your advantage. You can now utilize this strategy in stealth mode. Before, if you bid on Piazza or ARod, everyone knew what you were doing. There was no sneaking up on people. Now, it is less clear what the positions of scarcity are, so it is less clear which positions you might go after.

One advantage of this is that hardly anyone would know what you are doing until it is too late.

You actually can choose from many positions as long as you disguise your intentions. Elite outfielders have outpaced the next level by greater margins than in the past. The same is true at first base. You could load up on outfielders and first basemen in a strategy that would have flown in the face of scarcity strategists of the early 90s. One advantage of this is that hardly anyone would know what you are doing until it is too late. Most leagues count one or more DH or utility player in the scoring. Since outfielders and first basemen are generally the most productive, they tend to fill those utility spots on most fantasy teams. Owners like to fill out their infield before filling those utility spots, so they can maintain some flexibility. After they have filled their infield, they do not have to draft certain positions and their intentions

After you have made your list and ranked players by position, count how many players teams will need to draft to fill out their starting rosters.

are less clear to opponents. You can use this to your advantage. If you are satisfied with getting the 10th best shortstop and the 12th best catcher, you can let your opponents spend their money on more expensive infielders while you swipe the outfielders and first basemen. Your opponents will be alarmed to find that all that is remaining at first base are the likes of JT Snow and Scott Hatteberg. They were expecting much better to be available, but you changed that. By snapping up those power positions, you increase the bidding for lesser players across the board as illustrated in the hoarding section.

The beauty of this counterintuitive position scarcity strategy is that while you have planned to be weak in a few infield positions, your opponents will unexpectedly be weak in three outfield positions, first base, and however many utility positions your league has. Do the research on your league yourself. After you have made your list and ranked players by position, count how many players teams will need to draft to fill out their starting rosters. If you consider that outfielders, first basemen, and utility players are virtually interchangeable, you can count them as one category. In a 12-team league with three utility spots, first basemen and outfielders generally produce the best statistics so they will likely be drafted for those utility spots. Including the starters, that makes seven first basemen and outfielders. So 12 teams x 7 1B/OF = 84 outfielders/first basemen. When you are picking up the 12th best shortstop, your opponent could be drafting the 84th best outfielder/first baseman. The difference between the 12th best shortstop and the league's average, the 6th or 7th best, is probably much less than the difference between the 84th and the 42nd best outfielder/first baseman.

Spending Based Strategy

If you have been playing in the same league for a few years, you may have noticed that either the owners in your league tend to stick to published dollar values or the draft prices tend to fluctuate wildly depending on where in the draft they select players. You can take advantage of predictable spending trends.

If the teams in your league are very disciplined and stick to the commonly followed dollar values, when you pick up a player makes little difference. Therefore, you are free to either disguise your strategy from your opponents, or signal to your opponents exactly what you are doing. You may want to disguise your actions if you are planning to go after a relatively deep position like outfielder. You want others to spend some money and commit to investing in certain positions before you make any big moves so you will have less competition. A good time to pick an outfielder may be after a string of second basemen is picked. You also want to sneak up on people so you should spread out your outfield picks. You might pick up an elite outfielder, the 8th best second baseman, the 11th best third baseman, and then another top outfielder. You want to be involved in the bidding for players that do not fit your strategy; you just do not want to end up with them. Go ahead and bid on that top shortstop. Just bow out at a price you know would be a ridiculous bargain. If you end up with him, great, you can adjust accordingly. You want your opponents to think the presence of two great outfielders on your team was less strategy and more you getting carried away with the bidding.

If you notice that your league tends to overbid on the top players that come up at the beginning of the draft and some decent players go for $1 at the end of the draft, you will probably want to conserve your money so you have buying power over your competition when there are values to be had. Many leagues tend to operate this way and at least one owner tries to wait for bargains. In fact, it is common to end up wishing you had exercised more discipline and saved my money for the middle to later rounds. One caution with implementing this strategy is to make sure you do not wait too long. You need to have a few stars on your team if only for

If you wait too long, you will end up drafting many players with uncertain futures.

predictability. You know Sammy Sosa is going to hit home runs. You know Manny Ramirez is going to get RBIs, and Randy Johnson is going to have many strikeouts. When you get to players who are typically drafted in the middle rounds, you just do not know. Russ Ortiz won 21 games in 2003. Esteban Loaiza won 21 as well. These are good pitchers, but they are not sure things. It is possible that they have turned the corner in their careers and they will be perennial All Stars from this point on, but it is also very possible that they will revert to their career norms. If you wait too long, you will end up drafting many players with uncertain futures.

Roster Composition

Your goal is not to dominate a few categories, but to barely win or even come in second in many or all the categories. This is true whether you are in a cumulative scoring or a head-to-head scoring league. If your team ends up with 20% more steals than the next best team, you have done a poor job of optimizing your team's performance. If you discover that your team is especially strong in certain categories, you **must** trade your strength for strength in another category.

Punting a category is generally not a winning strategy. In Chapter 2, you read about the Tenacious Management Phenomenon where the teams that decide to go for the win almost always end up in the upper half of the league. Owners that decide they have no chance at winning this year either throw in the towel or optimize their teams for next year. The main reason why out of contention teams get even worse after their owners realize they have no chance of winning is apathy. The standings have little meaning to them. Free agent acquisitions are virtually useless to these teams. If the league has transaction costs for such moves, these owners may very well decide not to pick up players they know would help their teams in the standings. Most likely, owners who believe their teams are out of

> *You need to put your team in position to finish well in every single category.*

contention will not be aware of free agent players that could help their teams. They will not even be looking. The only reason for these teams to trade would be for keepers. By nature, teams giving up keeper players expect players in return that will help their teams this year. So on one side of a keeper trade is an owner trying to make his team better this year, and on the other is an owner consciously hurting his team's chances this year so it will be better the next. Teams trying to win attempt to optimize their free agency, roster, and trading transactions for this year. These owners manage their teams tenaciously. They will attempt to make moves that will give their teams the best chance of winning this year. Good teams get better and bad teams get worse. More accurately, teams whose owners think they are good get better, and teams whose owners think they are bad, get worse.

The same phenomenon holds true for each statistical category. Assuming your team has been in the hunt the entire year in the RBI category, after teams decide that they have no chance begin to drop out, your team, almost by default will end up in the upper half. This is not the case when from the beginning of the year, you decided to punt RBIs and draft a team of leadoff hitters. This is where the phenomenon will actually end up hurting you more than helping you. Assume the phenomenon holds true in every category. Your opponents, who are also going for the win, end up in sixth place or better in the categories in which their teams had been relatively weak. You however, will end up in twelfth place in RBIs no matter what happens. Those extra six points will be nearly impossible to make up in other categories against your strongest opponents.

You need to put your team in position to finish well in every single scoring category your league uses. Keeping the phenomenon in mind, you should consider the middle of the pack the absolute minimum score in any category if you are to have a chance at the end of the season.

Adjusting Mid-Draft

If you plan your draft strategy properly, your opponents will be the ones adjusting to your moves. There will still be times when you run into rough terrain and need to "shift on the fly". This is where you have to be flexible.

Anticipate

It is much easier to adjust when you have done some scenario planning ahead of time. Once you have laid out your core strategy, try to anticipate the moves of your competition and have alternative or supplemental strategies ready to implement. It is very difficult to come up with a new strategy during the draft. You have many distractions and you should focus on the bidding. A good overall strategy incorporates the draft, trading, free agency, management style, keepers, and more. Can you formulate a comprehensive strategy at a moments notice? Most people cannot, so they lose when the unexpected happens.

Remember the Fundamental Theorem of Fantasy Sports. When something out of the ordinary occurs during the draft, most people will manage their draft differently than they would have if they knew their opponents' strategies. If you have anticipated the shift in draft dynamics, you will be one of the few to gain from the situation. This is where having a strategy

Fantasy Baseball Strategy

that accounts for surprises will really set you apart from the rest. In those key moments during the season, you need to take full advantage. To better anticipate surprises and incorporate alternatives to take advantage of those surprises, you may want to ask yourself a few questions:

- Does your strategy account for surprises?
- What parts of your strategy are most likely to change?
- What would need to happen before you switched to an alternative plan?
- How will you adjust if these things occur?

Changing Valuations Based on Draft Conditions

Keep in mind that as the draft progresses, the values of players change. You may have carefully studied your magazines, downloaded projections, or spent hours devising your own valuation method tailored to your league. Those numbers may be very accurate, but after a few players are drafted, the valuations of the remaining players change. You may try to implement a strategy that alters the prices of players. Your opponents might even try to do so. Whatever happens, the valuations are constantly changing with each pick.

Know the Odds

You may be able to write a computer program that adjusts your player valuations after each pick. If you are not sure how to set one up, you can bring the *Adaptive Valuation Spreadsheet* to the draft on a laptop computer.[11] Short of that, the most practical thing you can do is to know how the odds are changing during the draft.

In Blackjack or Poker, a good player will reassess his odds as new information becomes available. Suppose you were playing Blackjack against only the dealer. Your goal is to get as close to 21 as possible without going over. You are holding a ten and a two of diamonds. The dealer is showing a king of clubs. She will probably have a decent hand when she is done because there is a good chance her hidden card is a ten or face card. There are 16 cards in a 52-card deck worth 10. You are at a disadvantage since a ten or face card will give you 22 if you hit and get one of them. With the available information on the board, you can calculate your odds of getting a ten or face card. There are 52 cards in a deck. Two out of 16 possible face cards or tens are showing. There are three cards showing so your odds of getting one of them and busting are 14/49 or 29%. Your next card is an ace. Now, a nine card will bust you too. Your odds of busting if you hit again are 18/48 or 38%. Still, it makes sense to hit since your odds of not busting are 62%. You hit again and get a seven to give you 20. You stay and turn your attention to calculating the dealer's odds of also getting a 20 when she flips her hidden card. There are 14 remaining face or ten cards in the deck so

> *The most practical thing you can do is to know how the odds are changing during the draft.*

---

[11] Available at www.fantasybaseballstrategy.com

her odds of getting a 20 are 14/47 or 30%. She gets a seven, has to stay, and you win.

From the Blackjack example, you can see that the odds are constantly changing as the dealer reveals each card. You can also see that with each face card or ten, the numerator and the denominator in the odds calculation changes. There is one less card worth 10 and one less card left in the deck. In fantasy baseball, each time a player is drafted, the odds also change. In this case, the odds are the expected prices of players. If there is a run of second basemen taken in succession, the prices of the remaining ones will change as rapidly as if the dealer turned over a succession of face cards in Blackjack. Your league may draft 24 second basemen out of 276 players. After one is drafted, there will be 23 left of the 275 players remaining.

In fantasy baseball, each time a player is drafted, the odds change.

Position Depth Knowledge

It is very important to know how deep each position is with worthwhile players. Let us suppose that you believe there are only eight shortstops worth drafting as your team's starter. You believe the other owners must feel the same way. You do not want to overbid because you just drafted two expensive players. You figure that your odds of winning the bidding on any one shortstop are about the same as any other owner's odds. If you think the price is too high, you will let a player go and try for a different one. Table 21 illustrates how the odds of drafting a player you deem acceptable decrease as the draft progresses. With no players drafted and 12 teams in your league, you have about a 67% chance of getting one of the eight acceptable shortstops. After about half the teams have drafted their starting shortstops, the odds of you getting one you want significantly decrease. This is because the demand is for 12 owners while there is only a supply of eight decent shortstops. The bidding for the final two players would be intense. You can fight the odds and overbid, but in that case, the other teams that have already drafted good shortstops gain, and you would lose.

Table 21: Odds of drafting an acceptable player

	Shortstops	Accept	Bidders	Odds
1	Alex Rodriguez	8	12	67%
2	Miguel Tejada	7	11	64%
3	Nomar Garciaparra	6	10	60%
4	Derek Jeter	5	9	56%
5	Edgar Renteria	4	8	50%
6	Orlando Cabrara	3	7	43%
7	Angel Berroa	2	6	33%
8	Rafael Furcal	1	5	20%
9	Alex Cintron			0%
10	Jimmy Rollins			0%
11	Rich Aurilia			0%
12	Christian Guzman			0%

To avoid getting into a bidding war with other owners for an acceptable player, you need to know each position's depth before going into the draft. This should also emphasize the need for organization during the draft. You do not want to pay a premium for players just because you did not keep track or you were not prepared. Here, the work you put into valuation is less important than the timing of your pick. Table 21 may display the players in what might look like ranked order. In your draft, especially if it is an auction, players will very well not go in order from best to worst. Alex Rodriguez quite possibly could be the eighth and final acceptable shortstop picked. Would you want to be in the position of either having to bid against five other owners for ARod or have a massive hole in your lineup? You do not, so you have to know to bid more aggressively when the odds are not stacked against you.

Imagine if one of your opponents used the hoarding technique in this scenario. It would dramatically shorten your odds of obtaining a suitable shortstop. Would you be able to adjust if someone did begin hoarding shortstops? It might be difficult, which is why you should become the catalyst and make people react to you. You can still adjust and get a fair price on a good player if you enter the draft with solid knowledge of position depth, are able to read indications of the changing environment, and remain flexible. Coincidently, those are the Characteristics of Champions from Chapter 1.

Overbidding and underbidding at the draft will distort your player valuations.

Price Inflation and Deflation

Besides the competitive aspect of bidding as the odds of getting a decent player decrease, overbidding and underbidding will distort your valuations. With a spreadsheet or database, you can keep track of how closely the prices of players are going for in your draft match your projected prices. By keeping track of relative overbidding and underbidding, you can adjust your player valuations accordingly. One simple, but inexact way to do this is similar to the way people count cards. In Blackjack, people count how many ten or face cards come up. You can compare the actual prices people pay versus your projected dollar amounts by counting during the draft. Keep a tally each time someone bids more than your projection, and a separate tally each time someone bids less. If there are more marks in the overbid column, you know the prices are inflated. If there are more in the underbid column, people have been paying less or prices are at a discount off your projections. This gives you an extra thing to do during the draft, but it could be quite rewarding.

> *If you can adjust your bets, as card counters do, to reflect the prices paid for players who have already been selected, you will gain a definite advantage.*

Remember, it is perfectly fine to act on "insider information" in fantasy baseball. Why do you think card counting Blackjack players are banned from casinos? It is because what they do gives them an advantage over the house. Casinos can lose money to these players because of their ability to count the cards they that have already been revealed. Who says you cannot "count cards" in your fantasy baseball league? If you can adjust your bets, as card counters do, to reflect the prices paid for players who have already been selected, you will gain a definite advantage.

If you are going to use a spreadsheet to keep track of picks and dollar amounts as part of your draft organization, the in-draft administration should be no more difficult than the tally method. It should be much more accurate and informative though. On a spreadsheet, you can have your projections for each player. As teams draft players, you enter in their actual draft amount next to your projection. It will be obvious whether each player drafted went for more or less than you had projected. You can then total up the results for each position. A snapshot of the totals during the draft will prove to be quite useful. An example of a summary page on a spreadsheet may look like the following table:

Table 22: Relative spending summary

Position	No. Drafted	Projected Cost	Actual Cost	% Change	Remaining Players	% Allocated	Remaining Dollars	Avg. Remaining
SP	12	$170	$240	24%	72	25%	$540	$8
RP	6	$90	$30	-67%	30	15%	$438	$15
1B	4	$100	$89	-11%	20	10%	$223	$11
2B	6	$114	$105	-8%	18	10%	$191	$11
SS	3	$90	$92	2%	21	9%	$173	$8
3B	8	$96	$124	29%	16	8%	$110	$7
C	5	$50	$61	22%	19	5%	$95	$5
O	14	$252	$240	-5%	58	20%	$368	$6
Total	63	$986	$981	-1%	254	100%	$2,139	$8

This summary provides you tremendous competitive intelligence. In this example, you now know that starting pitchers (SP) have been going for 24% more than you had projected. You expected that most owners would spend 40% of their money on pitching and 62.5% of that on starting pitchers. If those ratios hold true, teams will have an average of $8 to spend on each starting pitcher from that point in the draft on. If the first 12 pitchers had gone as projected, the average remaining pitcher might have gone for a dollar more. You can also see that owners underbid the relievers by 67%. That might indicate that your projections were way off. Even if they are, at least you have a system that can account for the difference. It could also just be a lull in demand because owners feel there are still plenty of alternatives remaining. It may be a good time to pick up some cheap relievers before things change. Surprisingly, overall, your projections are only 1% off. You may have weighted each position incorrectly though.

By keeping track of relative overbidding and underbidding, you can adjust your player valuations accordingly.

You might be able to do without such a tracking system to realize where the relative bargains are in your draft. It is all a matter of accuracy. Most owners would decide that preparing a spreadsheet like Table 22 and maintaining it throughout the draft is too much of a hassle. It could be. If someone in your league were doing something like it though, would he have an advantage over the rest of the league? Would he have an advantage over you? If the answer to either question is yes, this is something that you could do to manage your team better. It is up to you if you want to do so.

To save you the difficulty of setting up such a complicated adaptive valuation spreadsheet, it is available on the website[12] for a nominal fee. It will be much more affordable than software packages available elsewhere. Many of the processes are automated so you will only need a basic understanding of how to use a spreadsheet.

What kind of organization system will you bring to the draft?

Do you have a budgeting strategy? If so, what is it?

What kind of depth strategy will you have?

---

[12] www.fantasybaseballstrategy.com

The Draft

How can you keep track of the changing odds of getting the players you want during the draft?

How will you adjust your player valuations at the draft?

Chapter 8. Free Agents

Free Agents

Players picked up as free agent acquisitions during the season can provide a tremendous boost to your team. There is generally a great amount of luck involved when picking up free agents. By definition, teams did not expect players that become fantasy free agents to contribute much as of draft day. Any player of real value who is still available is probably going to be a surprise to everyone. So how do you strategize around an aspect of the game that is by nature unpredictable? You plan free agent acquisitions **before** the draft. To do that, you must know how your league's free agency rules will affect your ability to maneuver.

Anything Can Happen

There will be times when players perform at completely unexpected levels. In 2001, one team in my league made two of the best free agent acquisitions in memory on the same day. This team had an unusual amount of injuries in the first month of the year. He needed to replace his second baseman and improve his overall offense. He submitted relatively modest bids for two players who had been on a hot streak at the beginning of the season. One was second baseman Bret Boone, and the other was an unheard of rookie named Albert Pujols. These two lasted so long because of their records of accomplishment, or lack thereof. Bret Boone was entering his 10th season as a Major Leaguer. He had

> *So how do you strategize around an aspect of the game that is by nature unpredictable? You plan free agent acquisitions before the draft.*

pretty well established himself as a .250 hitter with 20 HR power, consistently producing between 60 and 70 RBI per season. He was not bad, just nothing special in a Mixed 5x5 league. Starting for a new team in one of the worst hitter's parks in the Majors, no one expected him to have a breakthrough season. No one in our league even knew how to pronounce Pujols, let alone tell you where he came from and what his credentials were. The Cardinals had not even advanced him to the upper Minor Leagues. Both Boone and Pujols were hot for a month, but many players get hot quickly and cool down just as quickly. These two never cooled down. Their final season statistics would end up being of historical proportions.

When putting together a plan for the season, you have to allow your team the flexibility to speculate on players who are hot and have the potential to stay hot.

Table 23: Boone/Pujols final season statistics

PLAYER	R	H	HR	RBI	SB	AVG
Bret Boone	118	206	37	141	5	.331
Albert Pujols	112	194	37	130	1	.329

Look at Table 23 and ask yourself if you could have used one or both of those players on your fantasy team. These free agents would have been among the best players in the league. These types of performances are rare to say the least, but you have to allow for the possibility that something similar could happen during the current season.

Boone and Pujols represent the potential quality of players that could be available as free agent acquisitions in any given season. That caliber of player could easily make your season. There is certainly a great amount of luck involved in picking up such players, but you still need to give yourself the opportunity to do so. When putting together a plan for the season, you have to allow your team the flexibility to speculate on players who are hot and have the potential to stay hot.

Roster Size

The impact free agency has on your league usually depends on the roster size of each team. Leagues with a long bench full of reserve players are less likely to have impact players left over as free agents. Leagues that allow for fewer reserve players will have quite a few quality players available in free agency. The effect free agency has is different in each circumstance.

In leagues with many reserve players, each team will have a few key reserves, and several reserves that are expendable. Suppose your team has 10 reserve players. Perhaps five of those players are actually quite good. Depending on match ups or who is on a hot streak, those five will occasionally see time as starters in your lineup. The other five reserves were late draft day pick-ups who seemed like they might have potential, but have not done much since. You are apt to have quite a bit of turnover with the last five reserves. There may be

> *The impact free agency has on your league usually depends on the roster size of each team.*

a dearth of talent available in the free agency pool, but you are confident that the five at the end of your bench will not see any playing time on your team and have little to no trade value. There is really no barrier to exchanging any of these players with free agents. Some leagues have limits – financial or otherwise – on free agent transactions, but in terms of roster sacrifices, there are few deterrents. The result is high turnover amongst your worst bench players.

With a small bench, there will be less bench turnover. Your team will have relatively good players on its bench. The opportunity cost of giving up one of those players for a free agent is large. It is also quite annoying to see one of the players you dropped acquired by a competitor. It is even worse if that player goes on to play a vital role on his team. As in our previous example, if your bench was only six players deep instead of 10, your options are limited. You have five key reserves and only one player who you could exchange for a free agent. In this case, you will wait for a free agent who you know will help your team. There will be more quality free agents available, but you have to be selective. The other owners in your league will be doing the same thing. When an obviously talented free agent bursts onto the scene, there will be intense competition for that player. Your chances of obtaining that player are slim.

When an obviously talented free agent bursts onto the scene, there will be intense competition for that player.

Before the draft, you should have a good idea of the roster constraints your league rules have on your team. If the constraints are severe, to optimize your ability to obtain the best free agents, you may want to draft for stronger starters and a few good reserves. That way you will have some open spots on your bench should an excellent free agent opportunity arise. If you know that you will have many reserve spots available, you might want to alter your drafting strategy to acquire greater depth. You should still have plenty of players you could release in order to take a shot at available free agents with more potential. In short, if you think you will need more flexibility to pick up free agents, you should concentrate your draft dollars on your starters. If you have enough flexibility, it makes sense to spend some more money on key reserves that you can rely on.

Position Planning

When planning your draft strategy, make sure that you think about the role free agency may play in filling out your roster. Budget constraints during the draft will force you to make tradeoffs. In order to get that star outfielder you covet, you will probably have to forego a top player at another position. You may decide that you are willing to take a lesser player at second base. After the top few second basemen, there is a sharp drop off in talent. After the first 10 or so, the remaining second basemen all have risks and limitations. Conventional wisdom says that even if you decide to get a lesser player at a position, the worst you should get is the 12th

> ***Conventional wisdom says that even if you decide to get a lesser player at a position, the worst you should get is the 12th best player as your starter.***

best player as your starter. After every owner has filled his starting spots for that position, owners start drafting reserves. If you are the only owner left without a starting second baseman and everyone in the league knows it, the rest of the owners might put the next best up for auction. They do this to force your hand so you have to pay the maximum for the 12th best player at that position. They do not want you picking up a starter for $1 very late in the draft.

Knowing that second base is a position where you can find a suitable player as a free agent can give you an advantage. Most owners only prepare to draft one starter and maybe one reserve at the infield positions. That means they usually do not prepare a list of players past 24 for any position – in a twelve-team league. If you plan your draft to account for the players you may pick up in free agency, you may have looked at the top 30 players for that position. It is quite possible that your analysis of the position shows that there is very little difference between the 10th best second baseman and the 28th. You know you are going to have one of the worst second basemen in the league. You understand that this allows you to be stronger in other positions. You also believe that if you do not get one of the top 10 players there, you will probably just end up exchanging your starter for a free agent at some point during the season.

You also believe that if you do not get one of the top 10 players there, you will probably just end up exchanging your starter for a free agent at some point during the season.

If you are going to replace your starting second baseman with a free agent anyway, you might as well spend the minimum amount you can during the draft, $1. You can allocate those extra dollars somewhere else. There must have been some reason why you have one player ranked 12th and another ranked 28th. This is true, but think of it a different way. If you spend $4 during the draft on the 12th best second baseman, there is still a high probability that he will be unproductive. You will probably end up cutting him and replacing him with a free agent. Consequently, you have thrown away $4 in draft money. Assuming half the teams draft a reserve second baseman, there will be 18 players gone and about 10 left that may be able to contribute to your team. Each of those 10 free agent second basemen has about the same or higher probability of being bad than the 12th best one you drafted. You have to assess the probability that one or more of those 10 free agents is actually going to put up some decent numbers. One thing is for sure, there will be some surprises.

You might as well spend the minimum amount you can during the draft, $1. You can allocate those extra dollars somewhere else.

Table 24 shows how the probability of one player out of the entire free agent pool exceeding expected performance is significantly greater than a single higher ranked player. This example comes from actual 2003 performances at second base. It is an illustration of how a plan to use free agency might alter your draft strategy. The 2003 Value column represents the actual earned dollar values of players ranked 12 through 28. Let us assume that having a starting player

Fantasy Baseball Strategy 175

contribute only $5.52 is an unacceptable level of performance for a competitive team. You want more, and $8.00 would be more acceptable. That would put your second baseman at about the level of an average team's starter. You know that in any given year, a player could perform much better than expected. In 2003 alone, Michael Young came out of obscurity and the shadows of two super-hyped teammates to end up as the fourth best second baseman in the Majors. Placido Polanco, Adam Kennedy, Frank Catalanotto, and D'Angelo Jimenez all surprisingly ended up in the top 12.

Table 24: Free agent upside probability

PLAYER RANK	2003 VALUE	PROBABILITY OF UPSIDE
12	$5.52	10.0%
13	$5.37	10.0%
14	$5.15	10.0%
15	$3.41	10.0%
16	$2.43	10.0%
17	$1.81	9.5%
18	$0.92	9.5%
19	$0.70	9.5%
20	$0.40	9.5%
21	$0.28	9.5%
22	$0.14	9.5%
23	-$2.20	9.0%
24	-$2.91	9.0%
25	-$3.33	9.0%
26	-$3.68	9.0%
27	-$3.75	9.0%
28	-$4.08	9.0%

Rows 19–28: 62% One Player

You think there is about a 10% probability that any given player will perform at a level of $8.00 or more. You just do not know which one. The odds are slightly less as you go down the rankings. With the 12th best player you drafted for $4, there is still only about a 10% chance he will give your team the kind of performance you need to be competitive. There is however, a 62% chance one of the remaining free agents will provide your team with the performance you want. This came from the calculation below if you want to check the math:

$$1-((.91)^6 \times (.905)^4) = 62\%$$

If one of those players performs at an unexpectedly high level as five second basemen did in 2003, your strategy can definitely work. The fact that five of the top 12 second basemen in 2003 unexpectedly broke into the top 12 suggests that the odds of any given player improving his performance significantly is much greater than merely 10%. What if the probability were higher that one of the top 28 second basemen would outperform? Table 25 is a sensitivity analysis for different assumptions:

Table 25: Sensitivity analysis of player upside

PROBABILITY OF A SINGLE FREE AGENT 2B EXCEEDING $8.00 IN VALUE	PROBABILITY AT LEAST ONE 2B RANKED 19-28 WILL EXCEED $8.00 IN VALUE
15%	80%
20%	89%
25%	94%
30%	97%

Fantasy Baseball Strategy 177

The table shows that if you assume there is a 15% chance of any one player – of the 19th through 28th - exceeding $8.00 in value, there is an 80% chance that at least one of them will do it. If you increase your assumption to 30% for any given player, there is a 97% chance that at least one will be worth $8.00. Given the 2003 actual performance of second basemen, 30% does indeed seem reasonable. Remember from *Figure 1: When in the draft to find values* from the Valuation Chapter, that drafted players only produce 52% of what was expected out of them. Where do you think that remaining 48% comes from? It comes from free agent players who exceed expectations. If you can accept 30%, that means it is virtually guaranteed a player not even drafted by your league will end up being one of the top seven or eight players at that position.

Beating Them to the Punch

Someone will outperform the expectations. It is almost a certainty. You just do not know who it will be. Just because it is certain that at least one player will outperform the 12th player drafted, it does not mean you will end up with him. You can however increase the odds that you will have more opportunities to find that one free agent player who will excel. At any given moment during the *You are competing against just a handful of other owners for a player at any given position.* season, a certain percentage of owners will not be looking for a free agent at the same position you are looking for one. Some will have star players who they would only replace in case of injury. Others will be happy with their incumbent player's performance. That means you are competing against just a handful of other owners for a player at any given position. If you wait until it is obvious a free agent is outperforming expectations, you will have more competition. What you need to do is be more active in your free agent acquisitions. When you see a player starting to get hot, pick him up. The optimum time to do this is before it makes sense for your opponents to do so. They have to consider whom they are going to drop to pick up that player. It may not be worth the risk if they are not reasonably sure a hot streak will turn into a full season's worth of achievement. To make sure you have the ability to implement this strategy of beating your opponents to the punch, you will need to structure your team appropriately.

Knowing that most teams will not always be looking for players at every position may pose an opportunity. If you look at free agents at all positions, even those where you are strong, you may be able to pick up a player only to trade him in the future. If a player is talented enough that he will eventually be picked up when a team has a need for the position he plays, you might as well gain from the transaction. Instead of letting your opponent pick up the player he wants directly, insert yourself as the middleman and extract a transaction fee. You may be able to make a minor trade that could be the margin of victory at the end of the season.

Opportunity Cost

The barrier to your opponents picking up that one player who will excel before you are able to is their opportunity cost. You have to make sure that when you draft, your opportunity cost is lower than your competition's is. This means that if you want to speculate on free agents, you need some place to put them. You need to free up roster space by spending more on your starters at other positions and spending very little on your last few roster spots. You can fill these spots with the best available player you can get in the draft for $1. If you have to drop those players, it is no big deal because you had little invested in them. Your opponents may have one roster spot with which he can speculate on free agents. If you have three or four, your odds of getting that one overachiever increase tremendously. You can acquire four second basemen from the free agent pool and put them at the end of your bench. Then play the one that is the hottest. One of them may just turn out to perform well all season.

Table 26: Opportunity cost of speculating

LAST 4 ROSTER SPOTS	YOUR TEAM	OPPONENT'S TEAM
1	$1	$5
2	$1	$4
3	$1	$4
4	$1	$1
Total	$4	$14

Your opponents cannot afford to speculate as you can because they did not plan for it in the draft. It would be much more costly for them because they incur greater opportunity cost. You can afford to speculate on four free agents because it will only cost $4 in opportunity cost. An opponent who did not plan to fill his second base position via free agency will incur a much steeper price. He will lose the performance of the released players. Those players ostensibly had a value of $14 during the draft. If he knew he was going to clear out four roster spots so he could speculate on second base free agents, he certainly would have spent that money elsewhere. Wouldn't that $14 have been better spent upgrading from Derek Jeter to Alex Rodriguez?

Wouldn't that $14 have been better spent upgrading from Derek Jeter to Alex Rodriguez?

In reality though, your opponents who did not integrate their free agency strategy with their draft strategy, will simply have to wait things out until they are reasonably certain a free agent acquisition will provide more value to their team than the opportunity they have to give up. If you plan your free agency strategy ahead, you can consistently beat opponents to the punch.

Player Movement

Players in certain positions change their status quite often. Perhaps the position with the most change is at closer. Few dominant relievers in the league are considered their team's undisputed closer. Many Major League teams do not have such confidence in any one individual. For this reason, there tend to be several free agent closers available throughout the course of the season. One strategy is to be conservative when spending money on closers during the draft. Unless you are getting a sure thing, you might end up wasting your money. Using the position planning strategy of beating other teams to potential free agents is a possibility. Pick

Fantasy Baseball Strategy 181

up set up men rumored to take over the closer role on their teams. You can load up at the end of the draft and through free agency expecting one or two to pan out.

This strategy applies to other positions as well. Some Major League teams struggle to stay profitable. These teams will often trade highly paid players midway through the season. The closer for Texas, leading the league in saves, may end up being the setup man in Florida. It has happened before. A team may trade its starting shortstop to the Yankees to be their utility infielder.

It is vitally important that you stay abreast of potential trade activity and position changes.

A veteran third baseman may lose his job to a young phenom the ownership group wants to display to potential buyers of the team. It is vitally important that you stay abreast of potential trade activity and position changes. Probably the best source for such news is ESPN.com in particular. Peter Gammons writes a regular column on all the rumors going around the league. He seems to be the reporter who is the most on top of things. If General Managers want to leak a rumor, they go to Gammons first.

Before setting your draft and free agent strategy, make sure to check the rumor wire around the league. Rumors are just that, rumors, but occasionally they turn out to be true. If there are multiple rumors involving different players at the same position, it may make sense to adjust your strategy so you will be in the best position to seize the opportunities when they occur.

Free Agents

So few drafted players actually perform as they are expected. How important will free agency be to your overall strategy?

How will you beat your opponents to the best free agents?

When position planning, can free agency fill some of your team's draft needs?

How will you keep up with the latest information about free agents?

Chapter 9. Trading

When you consider making a trade, the most important factor you should consider is whether your team will be better after the trade or not. Some owners refuse to trade with other owners they know are strong because they do not want to make them even stronger. This is understandable to some degree, but in almost every case, this practice is counterproductive. If you are able to help your team by making a trade, you should do it. If it just so happens to help your trading partner as well, so be it. In fact, it is desirable that your trading partner benefits, so he and others will be open to trade with you in the future. If it is blatantly obvious that your trading partner is getting the better end of the deal or his team is benefiting more than yours is, your best move is to negotiate a more equitable deal. It is not easy to consummate a trade. If you are close, you should do what you can to seize the opportunity.

It is desirable that your trading partner benefits, so he and others will be open to trade with you in the future.

Win, But Not By Too Much

The minute the draft is over; your goal is to make your team better via free agency or trade until the end of the season. To achieve this goal, you not only have to gain from each trade, you also have to facilitate future trades. Most owners bring an attitude to the trading table of trying to get the best possible deal. They will try to rip off their trading partner so they can trade away less value than they receive. They treat trading as an, "I win, you lose or you win, I lose" type

Fantasy Baseball Strategy   185

of transaction. The other owners judge most trades this way. There is usually a winner and a loser.

If the other owners in your league are competent, you should not be able to get much more value than you receive. In reality, everyone makes a bad trade occasionally. It still is not in your best interest to ask for the moon every time you trade. Each time you make a ridiculous offer, you shut down communication and lessen the chances of making a trade in the future that would be beneficial. If you try and try, eventually, you may succeed in bamboozling an opponent. What you will get in the long run is hard feelings, and a reputation as a con artist. This will limit your opportunities as well.

You want to make trading an efficient process of discovery. You want to share what you would like, and get an understanding of what your trading partner wants to accomplish through trading. Maybe your needs are compatible, maybe they are not at the moment. Once you discover what your trading partner wants or needs, you then have to gauge what he is willing to give up to get it. You do this by determining how he ranks his players. Suppose an owner in your league approaches you about a trade for your star catcher. In return, he will give you a star outfielder. You will also give him an outfielder and he will give you his current catcher to keep both of your rosters well balanced. He has quite a few outstanding outfielders to choose from including Sosa, Pierre, and Beltran. He offers you

Pierre, but you would rather have Beltran. You would love to have Sosa, but you doubt he would part with him. You are not a big Pierre fan and though you want speed, you do not think you need it that badly because you have an injured speedster coming off the DL soon. His offer of Pierre seems reasonable, but you decide to explore further to see if you could get what you really want. You inquire about how he rates his outfielders. His response is that he ranks them in this order:

1. Juan Pierre
2. Carlos Beltran
3. Sammy Sosa

That is good news to you because you rank his outfielders in the following order:

1. Sammy Sosa
2. Carlos Beltran
3. Juan Pierre

Taking the time to understand how your trading partner ranks his players and comparing it to how you rank them has uncovered a great opportunity. You could go straight to making an offer for Sosa instead of Pierre. Another route is to inquire about Beltran first. Since he values Beltran more than Sosa, he may be reluctant to talk seriously about Beltran. There is a strange thing that happens when someone else wants one of your players – that player seems a little bit better than before. It might be because someone else sees value that you missed. After talking about Beltran for a while, you give him your fallback position of accepting Sosa. You tell him that if you are going to take Sosa instead of Beltran or Pierre, you want a little sugar to sweeten the deal. You have him include a backup reliever to "even things out." In the end, you receive who you believe to be his number one outfielder, his starting catcher, and one of his reserve relievers for your star catcher, and an expendable outfielder. Your trading partner is happy because from his perspective, he got your starting catcher for his third best outfielder. Both sides win. The other teams in the league lose in relation.

You not only made a successful win-win trade, you demonstrated to yet another owner in your league that you are a reasonable and fair trading partner. In this regard, trading is very similar to trading goods on eBay or an online auction. A key selling point for you is your seller or buyer rating. Your reputation has a tremendous impact on your ability to make trades in the future. The entire league will know what your trading partners think of trading with you. Make trading with you easy and beneficial. You want your ex-trading partners to give you a call for another trade in the future. Even if you were unable to consummate the trade, you will have learned quite a bit about each other's needs, which may come in handy in the future. Every trade attempt brings you closer to consummating a future trade.

Incremental Improvement

You are not trying to rip off anyone. At the same time, you refuse to let anyone take advantage of you. If someone has to get the better end of the deal in terms of value, it will be you, but you should not attempt to gouge anyone. You want to make a fair offer so both teams involved in a trade will benefit. A trade may help one other opponent, but it should be fine with you if the two of you gain relative to the other ten teams. If everyone started out even after the draft, and you knew a trade would make your team 5% better and your trading partner 5% better, doesn't it make sense to pull the trigger on the trade? You have just elevated yourself to one of the top two teams in the league and greatly increased your chances of winning the whole thing. If you can keep making trades that incrementally make your team a little bit better each time, your team will be in a class by itself.

Making blockbuster trades, especially ones where you are perceived by the league to have gotten the best of the deal, tend to cause escalation. If it is obvious that you have helped your team, your closest competition will try to match you "tit for tat". It makes perfect sense logically. You improved your team so they need to also if they want to continue to compete. They will be looking to make a blockbuster too. An opponent may trade some of his keepers to an out of contention team that will net him a huge gain in talent. If you had not obviously improved your team by so much, he might have decided it was not worth giving up his keepers.

Focusing on incremental improvement will help you avoid sounding the alarm for your opponents to retaliate. You can also disguise your trades by focusing on position over value. If you trade speed for power, or an outfielder for a catcher it is not obvious that you improved your team. You will know what will improve your team far more intimately than your opponents will. If your opponents do not feel that you have absolutely improved your team, they will not feel compelled to respond in kind.

Position over Value

Trade for position over value, but try not to get ripped off. That means trading to position your team differently than how it currently is. It may mean trading an outfielder for a shortstop, or trading a power hitter for a speed player. If you improve your team because it improves the balance of your team by filling holes, fluctuations in performance will be of little concern to you. Your goal should be to improve your team. If your team benefits from a trade, you have succeeded. By focusing on improving your team by filling positions or categories it is weak in, you decrease the chances that you will be the "loser" of the trade. If you can devise a trade that will help you even if your trading partner gets more talent out of it than you do, you will be successful. Of course, you will try to get as much value as you can, but in some cases, that is simply out of your control. You

If you improve your team because it improves the balance of your team by filling holes, fluctuations in performance will be of little concern to you.

will never know with certainty ahead of time which players will perform the best after a trade. There is definitely some skill involved, but there is also a great amount of luck involved too. What you can control largely is which positions you fill via trade. If you have a platoon shortstop as your starter, but a surprisingly good extra outfielder on your bench, you have the makings of a trade. Trade those two to a team with two decent shortstops and you both win. You win because your team was losing considerable scoring from a part-time shortstop. Now you have filled all of your team's holes.

Uneven Player Trades

Trading talent for depth, or visa versa, is a legitimate reason to trade. Uneven player trades means the number of players each team involved in the trade gives up is different. Most trades are one for one or even player swaps. This is generally for convenience since most leagues have roster limits. Trading a number of players to another team for a different number of players is less common because it will usually necessitate more roster moves. A team receiving two players for the one he trades away will probably have to drop a player off his roster unless he happens to have an empty spot. The chances of a team having open roster spots is small because there is little advantage to keeping those spots open. It may not even be possible in some leagues.

The owner taking on more players than he trades away must factor into the overall value of the deal including the value of the players he must release. Conversely, the owner of the team taking on fewer players than he trades away should add the value of picking up a free agent. This creates an interesting dynamic that tends to make trades of this type seem lopsided to the other owners.

Table 27 illustrates how the other owners in the league may view an uneven trade to favor the team that

Fantasy Baseball Strategy 191

receives fewer players. You can see that if the players traded were exactly even in value, Team A actually gains more value from the transaction. He adds the value of any free agent added while Team B subtracts the value of any player he must drop because of the trade. This is of course assuming that the players traded were supposed to be even in value. Only the two trade participants know what they wanted to accomplish with their trade. Perhaps Team B was better able to fill holes in his lineup than Team A. At the very least, if you are involved in an uneven trade, you should be aware of the total trade value, not just the value of players traded.

Table 27: Value exchange of uneven trade

	TEAM A (Receives 2 Players)		**TEAM B** (Receives 3 Players)
+	Value Received	+	Value Received
-	Value Traded Away	-	Value Traded Away
+	***Value of Free Agent Added***	-	***Value of Player Dropped***
=	Total Value of Trade	=	Total Value of Trade

It may be easier to visualize with names of players you recognize. Suppose you decided to trade Mark Prior and Nomar Garciaparra for Kerry Wood, Edgar Renteria, and Braden Looper. Your team desperately needs saves and you think with the Mets, Looper might get quite a few more saves than before. You like Prior better than Wood, but you could use a few more strikeouts. Nomar has more power and he cost you a bit more at the draft, but Renteria has more speed, a category that you also need. Overall, it seems like a good deal for you. You gain in your three worst categories, and you are getting three quality players for two. You accept the deal. It seems like an even swap in terms of value, but you think it helps you because it positions your team better in the scoring categories. When you consummate the deal, the trade looks like Table 28:

Table 28: Initial perceived trade value

	YOU		OPPONENT
$27	Wood		
$19	Renteria	$37	Prior
$11	Looper	$20	Garciaparra
$57	Value of Players Received	$57	Value of Players Received

After the three-day waiting period, the trade goes through and you have to drop a player. You initially drafted a deep bench, so your free agent moves have not been easy all year. Your reserve situation got a little tougher when you picked up two highly touted minor league call-ups as free agents the previous week. You already had to make some difficult decisions, but your toughest player drop is about to come. You hate to do it, but you end up dropping Trot Nixon who had decent numbers the year before, but is off to a very slow start. You picked up Nixon at the draft for what you thought was a bargain at $8. Now he is gone and someone else will surely snatch him up as a free agent. Ironically, your trading partner ends up being the owner who picks up Nixon. He had a free roster spot from his trade with you so you should have known that he would try to pick someone up. The thought goes through your mind that you probably could have offered Nixon in the deal and possibly upgraded one of the players you did receive in the trade. The overall transaction now looks like this:

Table 29: Net trade value

	YOU		OPPONENT
$27	Wood		
$19	Renteria	$37	Prior
$11	Looper	$20	Garciaparra
-$8	*Nixon*	$8	Nixon
$49	**Value of Players Received**	$65	**Value of Players Received**

The other owners, knowing that your trading partner picked up the player you dropped, give you a hard time. Not too long ago at the draft, you valued the three players you traded away $16 more than the players you received in return. Have things changed that much? 33%?

The trade was actually a good one for your team, but it may not have been the best you could have gotten. In terms of player value, the other owners in your league could make a decent argument that you lost and your trading partner won. Your main goal was to trade for position over value. Your team will be more competitive in the league standings now. You are happy. Even though you did not make a perfect trade, you certainly did not get ripped off, and you incrementally improved your team. The other owners still give you a hard time though.

There is more to the perception that the team receiving fewer players usually gets the better end of the deal. There seems to be the common belief that it is harder to trade for talent than for depth. This probably stems from the fact that the best players on any given team are generally not subject to replacement by a free agent. Mediocre to poor players – those that tend to be on the bench – are more likely to have a free agent replace them. That is, they can more easily replaced by an inexpensive transaction.

Table 30: Irreplaceable talent

TEAM A	POINT VALUE	TEAM B	POINT VALUE
Alfonso Soriano	18.2	Mark Ellis	0.1
Replacement	0.0	Replacement	0.0
Difference	18.2	Difference	0.1

Table 30 shows that under no circumstances are you likely to replace a premiere player with a free agent. Soriano accounts for approximately 18.2 marginal category points for his team. Having Soriano instead of an undrafted second baseman is worth 18.2 points in the standings. The 19th best player at that position – assuming half the teams in the league keep a backup second baseman – does very little to help a team. He might even hurt a team. To exchange Soriano for a free agent second baseman, a team would have to make up at least 18.2 category points of offense somewhere else. It could certainly trade for value in another position to make up for the difference, but you could not afford to make the exchange via free agency. That much is obvious. Team B drafted Mark Ellis as the last second baseman taken. He neither helps nor hurts his team's standings much. In this case, a team could

Fantasy Baseball Strategy 195

easily exchange Ellis for a replacement player found as a free agent. The difference in offensive production is only 0.1 points. During the season, so much can change that 0.1 points can easily be within the margin of error. It is quite possible that a hot player you could pick up via free agency will even outperform Ellis. There is little to no opportunity cost for dropping him.

The last example was not exactly rocket science, but it does show what fantasy owners know intuitively when an uneven trade takes place. Unless you are trading for talent, you are probably better off exchanging your players for free agents. Trading for players that are not much better than those available via free agency is moot. Most reasonably knowledgeable fantasy owners know this and when they are involved in uneven trades, other owners think they are trying to confuse their less informed trading partners. Their distaste for uneven trades usually stems from an assumption that the strong is taking advantage of the weak. Others may not like to see uneven trades happen in their league, but that should not be your concern. You should not buckle to peer pressure and refrain from making an uneven trade if it makes sense to your team. Your best bet is to go on the belief that everyone in your league understands replacement value. They will make trades that are in their team's best interest. If you try to be magnanimous and point out all the nuances of replacement value, you will end up talking yourself and your trading partner out of a deal.

Gain Without Ever Making a Trade

It would be virtually impossible to draft a team, pay no attention to it all season, and end up winning. You have to be involved to a certain extent. Even after that disclaimer, you can gain even if you do not complete a trade. If you convince an opponent not to trade for a player you want, you gain. You do not want to make it your goal to hurt your opponents. You want to make the best trade for yourself, and if your opponent does well for himself, good for him. Sometimes trades just do not work out, but you have to be in the game. You need to keep your finger on the pulse of the league.

If an opponent is looking to make a trade, you want to be in the discussion. Knowing what is happening around your team is important, but staying involved has a more practical purpose. Even if you never make a trade, your presence in the negotiations will help ensure a lopsided trade between two other teams will not occur. Suppose Team A desperately wants to trade for a closer. He is close to making a trade with Team B, but you approach him just before he is about to make the trade official. What he is willing to give up strikes you as far too much. Thinking you would like to take advantage of such a generous offer, you may preemptively offer one of your closers for a similar deal. Even if Team A does not trade with you, at least he is aware that he has other options. He very well does not have to give up as much

The single most common reason for lopsided trades in any fantasy league is that the "loser" failed to shop his players around to other owners.

as he was originally offering to Team B. Your offer prompts Team A to shop his players to two other teams with extra closers. At this point, you have gained because you have altered the balance of power in your league. Without your intervention, Team B would have reaped the rewards of a lopsided trade and quite possibly surged ahead in the standings.

The single most common reason for lopsided trades in any fantasy league is that the "loser" failed to shop his players around to other owners. You need to stay involved in trading activity if for no other reason than to prevent a lopsided trade in your league. The more involved all the owners in your league are, the fewer lopsided trades there will be. Remember to shop your players around too. If trades result in an even swap of value, how you will gain is by trading for position. You are aware of this from the earlier section so you will come out ahead of the rest.

Types of Trading Partners

Know your competition so you understand how to approach them to get the most value out of trading. You also must know their tendencies so you do not fall prey to their tactics. As you read this section, it might be a helpful and entertaining exercise to write down the names of the owners in your league next to the different types of trading partners. It will help you identify their tactics earlier so you can get the most out of your dealings with them throughout the year.

The Romantic

Some owners fall in love with their players. This is understandable to a certain extent. The reason fantasy baseball is so popular is mainly because it keeps fans interested in baseball all year long. They follow players from every team, not just the local one. They know details the average fan just does not. It makes sense that you will care about the players you follow the most, the ones on your team. Romantics take this to the extreme.

This type of owner can be difficult to trade with because he values his players more than other owners who would like to trade for them do. It tends to make negotiations difficult because you have to sort through the seemingly irrational attachment.

One weakness of Romantic owners is that they have a special emotional attachment to certain players others do not. Many owners have a special affinity for a particular team or player. A transplanted New Yorker will usually value Yankee players a little more than your average Californian. The New Yorker will feel like a better fan if he has several Yankees on his fantasy team he can root for throughout the year. You will notice that certain owners have a tendency to overload their fantasy team with players from their favorite MLB team. This could be the result of a well thought out strategy because he knows more about his favorite team than others do. More likely, it is his romanticism coming out.

If you were going to try to use this knowledge to your advantage, it would be wise to pick your spots judiciously.

If you were going to try to use this knowledge to your advantage, it would be wise to pick your spots judiciously. Most romantics with team affiliations are aware of their weakness. It is no secret that they are fans of certain teams. During the draft, romantics will proclaim how well players from their favorite team are going to do this season. There are usually several other owners all too willing to point out his proclivity to overbid on players who wear his favored logo. This process usually sensitizes the Romantic to attempts by other owners to take advantage of his weakness. For this reason, it is usually best not to offer a Romantic one of his favorite players just for the sake of getting him to do something foolish. You should wait until you really want to make a trade. It would also help to identify how the Romantic's favorite player would nicely fill a need on his fantasy team. To stack the odds in your favor, you might wait until that player is especially hot, or has recently done something to help his team win in a dramatic fashion. Having a clutch player on your fantasy team means nothing to you, but it means something to the Romantic.

If you believe you are a Romantic, you should know a few things to minimize your mistakes. You cannot help being a fan. The best fantasy league managers are good because they love baseball. You should not lose that enthusiasm. You should however be aware of your tendencies to place too much value on your favorite players. Be careful to plan your draft and utilize the portfolio theory of roster composition. Romantics get into trouble when they accumulate one type of player. Usually, you will find that Romantics like to draft young players with lots of potential. What could be more romantic – in a baseball sense – than a relatively

Be careful to plan your draft and utilize the portfolio theory of roster composition.

unheard of player coming out of nowhere who suddenly becomes a star? Romantics will have more than their fair share of these players. They will "discover" a few bargains every now and then, but on balance, this practice usually hurts their chance to win more than it helps.

The Cold Caller

The fantasy league Cold Caller is the kind of owner who will contact everyone in the league. If he cannot quickly make a sale, he moves on to the next victim. Most owners do not like trading with a Cold Caller. It is not so much that they call during dinner; it is more that you know they are calling other owners. You get the feeling that any deal you negotiate will become the starting point for his negotiations with other owners. Because the Cold Caller will not commit, the time you invest in putting together a solid, fair offer is wasted.

When dealing with a Cold Caller, you have to make one thing clear; a deal is a deal. You should ask, "Is this a firm offer or are you just putting a toe in the water before you jump in with both feet?" Unless you get the sense that he is serious, you should refrain from making any firm offers yourself or investing too much time. You will know if he is serious when he makes a firm, fair offer. If the offer is firm but clearly unacceptable, you should not waste your time.

You can get a feel for the trading environment because you can bet that the Cold Caller has talked to several others before you.

Getting a call from a Cold Caller can be very useful. You can get a feel for the trading environment because you can bet that the Cold Caller has talked to several others before you. Usually, since just about everyone in your league is a friend, no one is going to lie to your face. If you ask him who else he has talked to and what they talked about, you can usually get enough information to tell if anything is imminent. Cold Callers like to say they are close to sealing a deal with someone else. They teach cold callers that kind of "urgency close" in Sales 101. If they say they are close, it is not the same as them saying they have an offer on the table. Keep asking questions until you have a feel for the trading environment, or until the Cold Caller hangs up. As you know, they do not like to do that.

If you are a Cold Caller, be aware of how you may appear to the other owners. They usually talk and know if you are talking to others about trades. If others believe you are trying to play them against each other, you will be in for a difficult time. You are liable to spend many wasted hours getting nowhere with trades on different fronts. Contacting the owners in your league is not a bad thing. When you do find a trading partner who wants to talk, deal with him earnestly. Give him your full attention. Be honest about where you stand in your negotiations with others and ask him to respect that process. Do keep everyone you have on hold informed of where they stand. If you deal with people openly and honestly, you should do just fine.

The Negotiator

The Negotiator tries to get as much out of you in a trade as he can. He views trading as a zero sum game. The less you get, the more he gains. The more you get, the less he gains. He tends to believe in the philosophy that a trade is a win-lose proposition and that win-win trades of the past were either bad trades or simply happenstance. You have to be careful of the Negotiator because he knows all the tricks of the trade. He will try to exploit any signs of weakness.

When dealing with the Negotiator, you can try to learn his tricks. If you have books on sales techniques or negotiation ploys, you will recognize what he is trying to do. It can actually be entertaining when you identify the technique he is using on you. You probably do not have the time or desire to learn all those new skills though. He has probably been a Negotiator for a lot longer than you have been. The single best thing you can do is know the players on your team and his. You should know what is fair and what is not. You might not though. Every year, in every fantasy league, there is someone who becomes a victim to the Negotiator and gives up more than he should have.

Every year, in every fantasy league, there is someone who becomes a victim to the Negotiator and gives up more than he should have.

What you can do when you are feeling the pressure of the Negotiator is to ask for a second opinion from another owner. Most owners in your league will not go so far as to sabotage a deal that you have in the works. Keep in mind that the second opinion you get may come from someone who has a stake in your deal not going through. This is fine. Sometimes you need a second pair of eyes to double check your work like an editor double checks an author's. The negotiations can go on for so long that

Fantasy Baseball Strategy 203

you can lose perspective. You may have had a clear objective for starting trade discussions, but the negotiations may have altered the deal so much, you lost your primary reason for trading.

If you are a Negotiator, try to trade for specific needs or positions instead of simply trying to get the most value. You can give up a little value and let your trading partner have a small win too. If you end up taking too much, the reaction from the other owners may hinder your chances of pulling off future trades. If you know a trade will benefit your team, it is in your best interest to speed up the process. Negotiators often find that they make fewer trades per season because their demands are higher. If you are unable to pull off a trade that would have helped your team, you lose. You can speed up the process by starting with an offer that is closer to where you would like to end up. Many negotiators believe that it is standard procedure to ask for more than you really want. They believe that others do the same and the negotiations will naturally work their way to middle ground. That is not the case. Sometimes, a final offer really is a final offer. Some people do not have the patience for a long, drawn out negotiation or will be offended. Either will end your chances to help your team.

The Persuader

The Persuader is someone who is always in your ear. The entire season is a negotiation. Persistence and charm are his best weapons. He usually targets certain players that he would like to transfer from your team to his. You can almost view the Persuader as someone who is a Romantic for your players instead of his own. The Persuader is someone who is dangerous to competitive teams because he may have been targeting a team all season that has fallen out of contention. One of the biggest fears of a fantasy league owner is to have another owner believe he is out of contention and hold a fire sale of his players. It becomes a feeding frenzy of owners trying to make the first deal. The problem is that the Persuader will usually get the first shot. If he has been talking to a team that has fallen out of contention, he will know before anyone when that owner thinks his team has had it. The Persuader also has the best chance of that owner buckling in to his persistence. If he is going to buckle at all, it might as well be to the person who has tried so hard all year to make a deal with him.

The opposite can also occur. If the Persuader falls out of contention himself, but has longed after another team's potential keeper player, he is liable to give in to any demands. He might trade away all of his expensive players who have no potential as keepers. His trading partner could receive a tremendous amount of value for the current season, by giving up the Persuader's favorite player who might help him next year. You do not want that since you are trying to win every year. Such a trade could shift the balance of power in the league to the owner the Persuader has been pestering all season. He gains big, so competitively, you lose.

The Persuader can be your ally. He can be your second opinion on other trade offers. As long as the players you are attempting to trade away are not the ones he has been targeting, you will probably receive an honest and thoughtful opinion. He does not want those players for himself, but he wants to get in your good graces so you will trade him the players he does want later. He may at times be an annoyance, but it is much better to have the Persuader trying to make a trade with you than it is to have him trying to make a trade with someone else.

If you are a Persuader, you will want to be careful not to become fixated on a select few players on other people's teams. You might miss other opportunities that are yours for the taking. You probably have a tendency to talk trade with the same people repeatedly. You might feel more comfortable with certain people, but taking a page out of the Cold Caller's book might be helpful occasionally. Expand your trade efforts to other owners and open up great new opportunities to use your charm.

The Apathetic

The Apathetic owner just does not seem to care much about trading. He does not seem very interested in the league in general. It is possible he is too busy or is new to the league. Either way, his apathy is cause for concern. It may get to the point where he simply does not care what happens to his team. He may have decided that the current season will be his last. You hope he will have the decency not to upset the integrity of the league and make a lopsided trade, but it does happen on occasion.

You should try to find out the source of the apathy. It could just be that his team is doing poorly and there is not much use in making trades. That may actually be a good thing for the league. When an owner thinks he is out of the race, it is probably best for the league if he remains inactive. If however he suddenly makes a trade, people start to question whether he meant to shake up his team, or to shake up the league.

This is a tough situation. You do not want to try too hard to trade with the Apathetic owner because it may upset the league. At the same time, if you make a decent offer and he later turns around and makes a much worse deal for himself, you will be able to call him on it.

If you find yourself becoming an Apathetic owner, your first responsibility is to your friends. Do not ruin their fun by destroying the integrity of the league with a blatantly unfair trade. If you cannot get enthusiastic about the league because your team has no chance, the fairest thing you can do is continue with your apathy and refrain from making any transactions that may upset the league.

The Unpredictable

This person's trading pattern is hard to predict. An example of the unpredictable owner is a Romantic who falls in love with his players. He may realize that he holds on to players too long because he likes them and becomes disgusted with himself. When his players do not perform to his satisfaction, like a jilted lover, he seeks a hasty separation. At this point, getting fair value is not his main priority; it is separating himself from the constant reminder of his obsessive stupidity. Unpredictable owners may make a very good trade on behalf of their team, then turn around, and make a very poor trade.

The Unpredictable owner is liable to do anything at anytime with his players. If you have identified an Unpredictable owner in your league, you may decide to act a bit more like the Persuader. You want to be around when he makes a wacky player personnel move. It is a little annoying to have

Fantasy Baseball Strategy 207

Unpredictable owners in your league, because you always have to stay abreast of their moves. You do not want another opponent gaining unfair advantage because of an extraordinarily poor move by the Unpredictable one.

If you are an Unpredictable owner, you probably know it just as if you were a Romantic. You can gauge by the feedback from all the rest of the owners when you make a bad trade. There is usually complaining. When there is an inordinate amount of complaining about you, then you will know. You can seek out second and third opinions on trades that you are planning on making. If the response is muted, you can probably trust your own judgment. If it is more along the lines of violent outrage, you know your trade compass is off kilter a bit. You can readjust from there.

Who is the best trader in your league? Why?

Why is it bad for anyone to get ripped off in a trade?

Trading

If you believe you can gain by trading for position over value, how will that affect the way you draft?

How will you factor in the players you drop or add via free agency into your uneven trades?

What are the trading styles of your opponents?

Chapter 10: Keeper Leagues

The trick to keeper leagues is to understand the potential trade value of keeper players and using that knowledge to balance between insuring that you are competitive for next year, and being competitive this year. Generally, you can trade your keepers with teams lower in the standings for players more likely to help your team now. There is a balance, but my preference is to shift the weight towards winning this year. There are very few guaranteed keeper players. If you have a chance to win now, go for it. You may not be in that position next year.

What is a Keeper?

Many fantasy leagues allow teams to retain the rights to players from the previous season. This helps maintain a team's identity over the years. Associating a player with a specific team or owner seems to create some continuity. It also alleviates owners from the feeling that they have to start completely from scratch each year. The presence of "keepers", players whose rights are retained, gives owners something to look forward to, long after the league results are a foregone conclusion. A team may fall out of contention early, but he can trade for keepers so he might have a better chance the next season.

Different leagues have different rules for keepers. Some leagues allow you to sign players to long-term contracts. You have to decide how much you think a player will be worth. If you think he will improve, you might decide to lock him up for several seasons. You can see that a side benefit of having keepers is that owners, who give up performance this year to invest in the future, tend to stay in the league. They want to experience the benefit they paid for in advance. Other leagues allow teams to keep a limited amount of players at a discounted or set price. This way, they are not subject to auction and lost to other teams. Some leagues allow teams to keep outright players at no additional cost.

The measure of a good keeper is not the absolute value of a player, but rather the net value. You would never trade Alfonso Soriano straight up for Aaron Boone. If however, Soriano would cost you $50 to keep next year and Boone would cost you only $4, Boone has a much higher net value as a keeper. Soriano probably would not even go for $50 in the draft, so you are better off not keeping him and bidding on him at the draft. Boone may be worth $12 at the draft so you could get him for an $8 discount.

No matter how your league accounts for keepers, the common denominator is that keepers present a tradeoff between optimizing performance now, and optimizing performance in the future. Knowing this, you can utilize your keeper rules to give your team a strategic advantage.

Later May Never Materialize

Teams will keep players that turn out to be great the next year. Nevertheless, most of the time, the hype is built into the price you have to pay. The players that end up being the best deals are ones that were originally drafted as afterthoughts who suddenly developed into valuable players that same season. When owners keep players for the next year is when the perceived value comes into play. For instance, a player drafted for $3 performed at a $15 level last season. This year, the team with his rights can keep him for $8. It would certainly seem that this team is gaining quite an advantage. The keeper value leaves quite a bit of room for error though. Much of that keeper value is in perception only. There are still many uncertainties regarding that player.

A spike in keeper value due to a dramatic performance increase by a player should be a warning sign that he is liable to experience an equally dramatic decrease in performance. Much as Miguel Cabrera of the Florida Marlins did in the 2003 playoffs, Anaheim Angels middle reliever Francisco Rodriguez gave a memorable and dramatic playoff performance. In the 2002 American League playoffs and World Series, Rodriguez became K-Rod because he was virtually unhittable. He made the best players on the best teams look like Little Leaguers. In 11 playoff appearances, the rookie with five innings of regular season Major League experience struck out 28 batters in only 18 2/3 innings. He also accumulated five wins - as many as all the Angels starters combined - while posting a 1.93 ERA. As a San Francisco Giants fan, I remember thinking, as he was mowing down hitter after hitter, that he was the best pitcher I had ever seen. His performance was so dominating that even with Troy Percival entrenched as the closer after his World Series MVP Award, the fantasy magazine with the largest circulation projected him to command a salary of $14. He seemed so dominant that eventually Anaheim would have to find a place for him in the rotation or as its closer. Fantasy team owners lucky enough to have him on their rosters probably could have kept him for the absolute minimum price. He

> *I remember thinking, as he was mowing down hitter after hitter, that he was the best pitcher I had ever seen.*

Fantasy Baseball Strategy

seemed like a great keeper. When K-Rod started the 2003 season with a 5.40 April ERA and a 4.40 May ERA, many fantasy owners who kept him the entire off-season as their prime keeper player, summarily dumped him into free agency. He turned his season around, but was about as valuable as any middle reliever – not very in most leagues.

Derek Lowe of the Boston Red Sox was another player who appeared to be a tremendous keeper prospect, but ended up being a bitter disappointment to his fantasy owners. After a difficult 5-10 season in 2001, the converted reliever could have been drafted for less than $5 in most leagues. The 2002 season turned into what seemed to be a breakout year for Lowe. He produced 21 wins, a 2.58 ERA, and a miniscule 0.97 WHIP.

According to that same popular magazine, Lowe's 2002 performance was worth $36. As a keeper, most fantasy owners knew not to expect a repeat performance, but he had dominated the league for an entire season. The magazine gave Lowe a $29 value going into the 2003 season. Two experts in another popular fantasy magazine picked Lowe as the "Safest $15+ AL Starting Pitcher." Representing about a 900% increase in value, Lowe was about as good of a keeper as it gets – at least it seemed that way at the time. His actual 2003 numbers were 17 wins, a 4.47 ERA, and a horrendous 1.42 WHIP. Projected to be a top 10 pitcher by nearly every fantasy valuation source

Few teams would have the resiliency to recover from such a let down equally dramatic decrease in performance.

to start the year, ESPN.com's *Player Rater*, ranked Lowe only the 82nd best pitcher in the Majors.

Table 31: Perceived value fluctuation

PLAYER	2002 DRAFT	2002 ACTUAL VALUE	2003 DRAFT	2003 ACTUAL VALUE
F. Rodriguez	$1	$0	$14	$3
D. Lowe	$3	$36	$29	$5

Figure 4: Keeper inflation and deflation

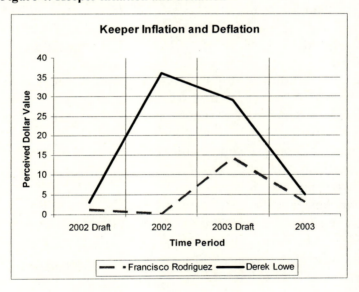

Fantasy owners might not have even drafted him had they known what he would do. While 17 wins is a nice total, he pitched on the best offensive team and received 7.26 runs per game in support – the most in the Majors. The wins kept him in fantasy teams' lineups all

Fantasy Baseball Strategy

year long while his ERA and WHIP demolished their chances. It must have been more painful to his owners who planned their pitching staffs around already having a top pitcher on their team before the draft had even started. Unless they drafted an unusually strong pitching staff, few teams would have the resiliency to recover from such a let down.

What happened to many fantasy teams who kept Derek Lowe at a perceived bargain should be a reminder of what can happen when players come out of nowhere. Players come out of nowhere and often go back to nowhere.

Option Pricing

You can look at keeper players as if they were stock options. The purpose of discussing the stock option valuation method is not to confuse you. It is to let you know that there are models out there for valuing your options as a fantasy owner. You can choose to approach your fantasy baseball options in a scientific way if you choose to do so. This explanation of the correlation between stock option valuation and fantasy keeper valuation will be in concept as opposed to the actual method. Please refer to the Black-Scholes Option Pricing Model if you want to explore the relationship further.

In short, the way to value stock options in the financial markets is to determine the value of the underlying asset and to determine the time value. If you own an option to buy 100 shares of Microsoft stock for $40 each (the strike price) and the price of the stock (the underlying asset) goes up to $50, the value of your option increases. In fantasy baseball, the expected value of your keeper player (the underlying asset) in the draft next year will increase or decrease in correlation to that player's performance this year. The time value of an option takes into account the possibility that circumstances change over time. The shorter the period, the less likely things will change. The longer the option, the more likely they will change. In the stock market (but not in fantasy baseball), there is the assumption that over time, stocks will generally increase in value. Therefore, the longer the option is good for, the greater the time value. If you own an option that expires in one month, not much is likely to happen in that timeframe. If the option is good for three years, there is a good chance that something, presumably positive, will happen. The change could be positive or negative though. The longer you have to decide, the more time value you have. For your player, you want to estimate the range of that possible change. If there is more upside than down, a longer period is better than a short one. If you expect that there is more downside, a longer period may be undesirable.

Table 32: Stock option valuation

OPTION TYPE	STRIKE PRICE	ASSET VALUE	TIME VALUE	OPTION VALUE
Stock Option	Buy Asset at $40	$50	20%	$60
Stock Option	Buy Asset at $40	$50	-20%	$40
Stock Option	Buy Asset at $40	$30	20%	$36
Stock Option	Buy Asset at $40	$30	-20%	$24

Fantasy Baseball Strategy

With a stock option in Table 32, the price of the underlying asset can be higher or lower than the strike price. The strike price is the price at which you have the right to buy the asset (the stock). The higher the asset value, the more the option is worth. Whatever the asset price is at any given time, there is still a chance that it will change over time. The table shows how a 20% change in value over time will affect the overall value of the option. The value of the option is that if the asset increases over time for $40 to $60, you can buy it for the strike price of $40 and make a $20 profit. If the asset decreases in value over time to $20, you do not take a $20 loss; you simply choose not to exercise your right to that stock. All it cost you was the cost of the option itself.

Whatever level he is performing at, by the time of the draft, changes affecting his performance may occur.

Table 33: Fantasy keeper valuation

OPTION TYPE	KEEPER PRICE	CURRENT VALUE	TIME VALUE	KEEPER VALUE
Keeper	Draft for $6	$20	20%	$24
Keeper	Draft for $6	$20	-20%	$16
Keeper	Draft for $6	$15	20%	$18
Keeper	Draft for $6	$15	-20%	$12

In fantasy baseball, calculating the keeper value is very similar. You know how much you can keep a player for in the draft next year. How much that player will be worth at the time of the draft depends on his performance this year. In Table 33, you have two values for comparison. In this example, the player you have the right to keep is either performing at a $20 level, or a $15 level. Whatever level he is performing at, by the time of the draft, changes affecting his performance may occur. This is the time value. The example shows what would happen if he gets 20% better than he is now versus 20% worse. When you factor in his current value and the time value, you get a range of draft values for that player.

Having the right to keep a player for the next season is similar to having the right to purchase a stock with a stock option. You retain the option on keeping a player all off-season. If something adverse happens to decrease the value of the player, you may not have to exercise your option to purchase him. That of course depends on your league keeper rules. Just realize that over time, things can change. What a player does in one season is not equal to what he will do in the future.

Keeper Trades

A player's value may never be greater than it is as a potential keeper. A hyped player can generate tremendous trade leverage for a team. In many cases, an unproven player who has potential as a keeper will be worth more than a proven star. Derek Lowe at his peak 2/3 of the way through the 2002 season could have commanded a tremendous amount as trade bait. Fantasy owners could have easily traded him to a non-contending team for another top pitcher and probably another good player as well.

It is difficult to trade away a player that presents such a tremendous potential value the next season.

Fantasy Baseball Strategy 219

It is difficult to trade away a player that presents such a tremendous potential value the next season. But, if you have the opportunity to trade a keeper for players you are certain will help your team contend or even win your league, you should probably make that trade. There is quite a bit that can happen in the six months between seasons. In Lowe's case, he battled skin cancer. He had minor surgery on his nose, to have the growth removed, but his concern may have affected his performance on the field. Maybe the cancer had no effect, but something definitely changed with Derek Lowe.

If you have a trade opportunity that presents you a known present value, for an equal unknown future value, take the known if it will help you win. You have to discount the future. Lottery winners have a choice of taking $100 million over 20 years or $25 million in a lump sum immediately. Most take the money now. All things being equal, so should you.

If you can receive established star value by trading a keeper, you are optimizing the management of your team.

Certainly if your team is out of contention or far ahead of the competition, you want to keep the players that present the greatest value to your team. You just do not want to pass up an opportunity to win for the chance to keep a player who might help you be in the position to win next year. Win now, and adjust later.

Another thing to keep in mind when considering a trade of a keeper is where his perceived value is on the scale. If a player is trading at or near his terminal value, you should attempt to trade him away. Terminal value means a level where he could hardly bring more in return. Derek Lowe was at terminal value 2/3 of the way through the 2002 season. He had pitched in enough games to prove to any skeptics that his dominance was no fluke. When other owners talked about him as being on par with established star pitchers, that should have been considered a warning signal. He may have been a star pitcher at that point in time, but 2/3 of a season or even one year does not make him "established." If you can receive established star value by trading such a player, you are optimizing the management of your team. Just as in the stock market, you want to buy low and sell high when you trade.

Managing Your Keepers

If you are fortunate enough to have a good keeper, your team is in a position of power. Every team in your league would want a good keeper, but at least half of the teams in the league will be serious about trading for such a player. The things to consider when deciding what to do with keepers are:

- Your position in the league this year
- The demand for your keeper
- How long he will remain a bargain
- The probable draft value of the player
- The probable actual value of the player
- The amount of uncertainty about his future

The first test when deciding what to do with a keeper is assessing your team's position within the league. There are only two reasons to trade a keeper player – to improve your standings in the league this

Fantasy Baseball Strategy 221

year, or to obtain different keepers. If you want to trade keeper for keeper, trust your judgment. If you are trading to improve your team's standing in the league, you really have to think hard about your chances. There is not much sense in trading away strength in the future when your team is hopelessly out of contention. Consider the demand for your keeper. Will the demand subside? Is the hype surrounding the player warranted? Are there special circumstances that make the player unusually attractive? Dontrelle Willis became a phenomenon across baseball for the 2003 World Champion Florida Marlins. He was an excellent pitcher and deserved his Rookie of the Year Award. The reason why he won the award was not that he was the best rookie performer in terms of fantasy statistics. There were at least a couple of players with better fantasy numbers. He won the award because he inspired his team by becoming its leader in many ways. He became a cultural and social phenomenon, bringing interest from the fringes of baseball. As great as he was for baseball, cultural, social, and inspirational leadership mean very little to a fantasy team. The hype surrounding a player like Willis can create enough interest and demand among the other owners in your league, that you will be able to trade him for more than he is really worth.

How much would your keeper go for if he were available to everyone in the draft?

How much would your keeper go for if he were available to everyone in the draft? You have to know the answer to such a question to know what kind of value others might pay for that player. Having an idea of your keeper's expected draft value will also let you know how much of a bargain he would be if you kept him. Sometimes that expected draft amount could be different from the expected value during the next season. You have to factor in how much things can change. Remember that your goal is to determine what the expected values for next year would be this year.

You also want to determine if the player you are considering is going to be a keeper for more than one year. If you expect him to be a bargain for two or even three years, you have to weigh that against trading for the present. Do you want to decrease your chances for the next three years for a chance this year? You might not want to take that risk. Just keep in mind that you will not always be in position to win your league. There will be times when your team experiences major injuries to key players. You can only control certain things. Having a chance to win 75% of the time would indicate you have done your job as a manager.

> *Keepers present a tremendous value proposition to teams that are out of contention.*

Drafting for Keepers

Now that you know what is involved in trading and valuing your keeper options, you can incorporate that knowledge into your draft strategy. You know that keepers present a tremendous value proposition to teams that are out of contention. They will be willing to give up more talent in the present for a chance at improving their team in the future. This is an area where you can create value for yourself. By choosing to draft young players with upside potential over solid, predictable players as your reserves, you can consciously attempt to improve your buying power at the draft.

Many fantasy owners will draft players with keeper potential, but do not have a solid plan for using them to compete in the current year. If you are going to forgo the predictability of having solid reserves, you have to go into the draft believing that you will eventually trade your players that turn into keepers. Deciding mid-season that you are going to keep them will cost your team the value of a bench that would have supported your team's needs better before the trade. This is because if you draft five potential keepers, one may turn out to be very good. The others will probably not be very useful to your team, especially in the early portion of the season. Young players with potential are not keepers if they have already proven they can contribute immediately. You are able to draft them inexpensively because they still have a lot to prove.

They will be willing to give up more talent in the present for a chance at improving their team in the future. This is an area where you can create value for yourself.

Do you know of teams in your league that always seem to have the best keepers, but still cannot win?

_____
_____
_____
_____
_____

Are you planning to trade away the keepers you consciously draft?

How will you evaluate your keeper options?

Chapter 11: Putting It All Together

Putting It All Together

Now that you have read the different fantasy baseball strategies, you can start to formulate your own. You will want to start with a core concept that you can refer back to so you can stay focused. It might be The Fundamental Theorem of Fantasy Sports, or it could be Porter's attributes of sustaining competitive advantage. It could be something different all together. Next, you will want to pick or create strategies for the main elements of fantasy baseball. You can use the chapter headings to guide you. When you have filled out your strategies, you should draft some alternative strategies should you need to change some of the elements due to surprising circumstances. Once you have your strategies, do some tactical planning. Create the spreadsheets, make your lists, determine the depth levels, and organize how you will implement your strategy on draft day.

I have prepared a list of questions that you should be able to answer once you have developed your strategies. You should use this list of questions as a checklist. If you can answer these questions easily and more thoroughly than your opponents can, you will surely put your team in a position to win your league. Remember, you cannot control everything. You may be unlucky one year, but if you approach your league with solid strategies, you will eventually prevail. Reading over the questions first may help to reinforce what you have learned throughout this book. They may also be a good reference to help you formulate your strategies.

Another way to gauge your readiness is to rank how well you can answer each question. Next to each one, rank yourself from 1-12 (or however many teams are in your league). If you are confident that you can answer the questions better than anyone else in your league can, give yourself 1 point. If you think you are at about the same level as everyone else, give yourself a 6 or 7. If you have no clue, or your strategy does not account for it, give yourself a higher number. When you are done with all the questions, take the average to see how you might rank against the toughest competition in your league.

Strategy Checklist

CHARACTERISTICS OF CHAMPIONS	RANK
• What is your knowledge level compared to the other owners?	
• How good is your ability to read the indicators other owners give off?	
• Can you maintain flexibility with your strategy?	

FUNDAMENTAL THEOREM OF FANTASY SPORTS	RANK
• How well does your strategy adhere to the theorem?	

COMPETITIVE STRATEGY	RANK
• Is it in your opponent's self-interest to help you?	
• Does your strategy force your opponents to react?	
• Does your strategy create value opportunities?	
• Does your plan contain the five attributes of sustaining competitive advantage?	

• Is cost leadership a crucial part of your strategy?	
• How well is your strategy differentiated?	
• Would you bet on yourself to win?	

PLAYER VALUATION	RANK
• Do you know what others are looking at?	
• Are your player valuations adjusted to the specifics of your league?	
• Do you know what your team needs to win in each category?	
• How close to a winning team can you get at the draft?	
• Do your dollar values account for ABs and IPs?	
• Where and when will you find bargains during the draft?	

SPECIAL CONSIDERATIONS	RANK
• Are there underappreciated positions in your league?	
• How much will you spend on starters and relievers?	
• Do you account for injuries among starting pitchers?	
• What pitcher characteristics will you have on your team?	
• Will you avoid drafting a team around specialists?	
• Which players have unique statistical characteristics?	

YOUR MANAGEMENT STYLE	RANK
• Do you know your style?	
• Do you know your competition?	
• Does your drafting strategy support your style?	

THE DRAFT	RANK
• Does it matter if your league has an auction or draft?	
• How well organized are you for the draft?	
• Will you be drafting for depth or star power?	
• How will your depth affect your trading ability?	
• Risk insurance. Do you have any?	
• Will you be hoarding? How will you react if someone else does?	
• Can you adjust to changing player prices better than the rest?	
• Can you pile on if another owner chooses a complementary strategy to yours?	
• Predictability has a value. Whom can you rely on?	
• Are you aware of position scarcity and the talent levels at each position?	
• Are you drafting for scarcity?	
• Do you have a spending based strategy and budget discipline?	
• Does your team have any holes?	

FREE AGENTS	RANK
• Are you ready for surprises?	
• Does your roster size dictate your free agent strategy?	
• When position planning, are there good alternatives in free agency?	
• Can you beat them to the punch by reducing your opportunity cost?	
• Can you save by acquiring free agents whose status could change?	

TRADING	RANK
• Do you trade to win, but not too much?	
• Do you strive for Incremental Improvement with each trade you make?	
• Will you trade for position over value?	
• When making uneven player trades, do you take into account players that need to be dropped?	
• Do you know how to gain without ever making a trade	
• For which players do the Romantics pay more?	
• Does the Cold Caller keep you informed?	
• Will you get a second opinion when dealing with the Negotiator?	
• Can the Persuader help you trade with other teams?	
• Why is the Apathetic that way?	
• Are you on the Unpredictable owner's list of trade partners?	

KEEPERS	RANK
• Do you manage for this year or the next?	
• Are you getting all the trade leverage out of your keepers that you can?	
• Do you manage your keepers as you would stock options?	
• Are you going to draft keepers to trade or to keep? Decide now.	

Worksheet for Strategy Development

When filling out the Strategy Development Worksheet it should be general enough to be clear in your mind. At the same time, you should have enough specificity to guide you in your preparation and implementation. Fill out the boxes to describe your strategies for each main strategic area. When you have completed each box, be sure to explain the linkage between strategies. Doing so will insure that you have a comprehensive, integrated overall fantasy baseball strategy.

MY OVERALL STRATEGIC CONCEPT IS:

LINKAGE:

Fantasy Baseball Strategy

MY COMPETITIVE STRATEGY IS:
Create Value, Differentiate
Alternative Strategy:

LINKAGE:

MY STRATEGIC VALUATION ADVANTAGE IS:
Adjust for league, find bargains
Alternative Strategy:

LINKAGE:

234 *Putting It All Together*

SPECIAL CONSIDERATIONS TO LOOK OUT FOR:
Underappreciated, specialists
Alternative Strategy:

LINKAGE:

MY MANAGEMENT STYLE SUPPORTS MY STRATEGY BY:

LINKAGE:

Fantasy Baseball Strategy

MY DRAFT STRATEGY IS:
Organize, make others adjust, depth, spending
Alternative Strategy:

LINKAGE:

MY FREE AGENT STRATEGY IS:
Roster size, position planning
Alternative Strategy:

Putting It All Together

LINKAGE:

MY TRADING STRATEGY IS:
Incremental improvement, opponent types
Alternative Strategy:

LINKAGE:

MY KEEPER STRATEGY IS:
How many, leverage
Alternative Strategy:

Fantasy Baseball Strategy

Strategy Aids and Resources

Visit www.fantasybaseballstrategy.com on the web for additional information.

- Software to help you prepare for the draft
- Tools for honing your valuations to match your leagues specifications
- Draft software that adapts to the changing conditions of your auction and alters the valuations for the remaining players with each pick

Other Online Resources

The following resources are more than enough to keep you up to date with the latest baseball news and analysis. This is far from an exhaustive list, but it covers all the bases.

- **Fantasy Baseball Links**
  Links to the leading fantasy and rotisserie websites
  http://www.fantasybaselinks.com/

- **ESPN's Fantasy Baseball Page**
  News and analysis
  http://games.espn.go.com/cgi/flb/frontpage#

- **Sporting News Fantasy Source**
  News and analysis
  http://fantasy.sportingnews.com/baseball/home.html

- **USA Today Fantasy Baseball**
  News and analysis
  http://fantasybaseball.usatoday.com/index.php?sport=bsball

- **Fantasy Baseball Café**
  Fantasy Baseball Discussion
  http://www.fantasybaseballcafe.com/

- **The Roto Times Baseball Page**
  Projections, Local Newspapers
  http://rototimes.com/index.php?sport=bsball&type=home

- **Baseball Prospectus Online**
  Statistical Baseball Analysis
  http://www.baseballprospectus.com/

- **CBS Sportsline Fantasy Commissioner**
  League Administration
  http://fantasy.sportsline.com/

Thanks for choosing
Fantasy Baseball Strategy

I would enjoy hearing from you.
Please send comments or questions to:

book@fantasybaseballstrategy.com

Henry Lee
Squeaky Press
P.O. Box 4452
Mountain View, CA 94040-0452

Index

A

Accounting for Reserves · 4, 69
Active Manager · 119
active trader · 122, 126
Adaptive Valuation Spreadsheet · 62, 157
Adjusting for your League · 3, 52
Adjusting Mid-Draft · 4, 156
adjusting valuations · 55
Alex Rodriguez · 41, 52, 58, 59, 61, 62, 114, 139, 160, 161, 180
allocation · 65, 78, 79, 83, 84
American Journal of Sports Medicine · 86
anticipate · 18, 19, 29, 118, 156, 157
approach · 12, 13, 97, 118, 196, 197, 215, 226
auction · 13, 51, 74, 126, 127, 129, 131, 140, 143, 147, 161, 173, 187, 211, 229, 237

B

barrier · 171, 178
Barry Bonds · 58, 59, 60, 61, 62, 112, 128
baseball news · 51, 237
Beating Them to the Punch · 5, 177
Bet on Yourself · 3, 39
bidding · 13, 46, 75, 84, 128, 138, 140, 143, 151, 153, 156, 159, 160, 161, 211
Billy Wagner · 112
Blackjack · 158, 159, 162
blockbuster trades · 188
books · 8, 10, 202

bottom line · 12, 82, 83
breakout seasons · 133
Bret Boone · 168
budget · 49, 64, 65, 69, 79, 89, 229
Buy and Hold · 118

C

Cal Ripken · 145
Case Study · 3, 4, 30, 107
category value · 57
characteristics · 16, 19, 20, 94, 109, 115, 116, 228
closers · 91, 93, 103, 104, 112, 135, 143, 180, 196
CNNMoney · 8
Common Arguments Refuted · 4, 83
Common leagues · 57
Commonly Used Resources · 3, 48
Competitive Advantage · 3, 36
competitive strategy · 36, 74, 137, 141, 233
comprehensive strategy · 14, 39, 41, 118, 156
control pitchers · 100, 101
Conventional wisdom · 172
cookie cutter strategies · 10
Cost Leadership · 3, 38
Curt Schilling · 99, 110, 123, 143
Cy Young · 94, 100, 111, 142

Index

D

Depth to Support Your Strategy · 4, 134
Derek Lowe · 213, 215, 218, 219, 220
Differentiation · 3, 39
Disabled List · 85
discount · 113, 141, 162, 211, 219
dollar value · 40, 47, 52, 54, 63, 64, 147
Draft day · 127
Draft Type · 4, 126
Drafting for Depth · 4, 131

E

entrance fee · 9
Eric Karabell · 51
ESPN.com · 8, 48, 51, 181, 214
expected values · 222

F

fantasy baseball leagues · 9, 126
Fantasy sports industry · 9
Fantasy Sports Trade Association · 9
Finding the Right Mix · 3, 65
Flexibility · 3, 18, 19
Francisco Rodriguez · 212
free agent acquisitions · 36, 39, 168, 170, 178
Fundamental Theorem of Fantasy Sports · 3, 6, 21, 27, 29, 30, 33, 34, 53, 144, 156, 226, 227

G

gamesmanship · 126, 128
General Manager · See GM
GM · 11

H

head-to-head · 59, 154
historical · 54, 55, 169
Hoarding · 4, 43, 137

I

Incremental Improvement · 5, 187, 230
Indicator reading · 17
Insider trading · 23
Insurance · 4, 131, 136
interchangeable · 13, 122, 151

J

Juan Pierre · 107

K

Keeper · 210
Keeper Trades · 5, 218
keeper value · 212, 217
key reserves · 170, 171, 172
Know the Odds · 157
Knowledge · 3, 5, 16, 24, 159

L

Larry Walker · 114

leading base stealers · 6, 105, 106
lopsided trade · 196, 197, 205
luck · 25, 26, 27, 107, 133, 168, 170, 189

M

Maddux · 100, 111
magazines · 8, 9, 16, 38, 40, 47, 50, 51, 52, 103, 129, 157
Major League Baseball · 11, 85, 92, 93
marginal · 25, 54, 59, 64, 65, 66, 75, 149, 150, 194
Maximizing Starts · 121
mechanics · 94, 97, 98
Michael Porter · 36
minor league phenoms · 75
Mixed 5x5 Fantasy league · 13
Moneyball · 68
multiplier · 63, 71

N

nature of pitching · 62
Net trade value · 6, 193

O

on-base percentage · 68
online leagues · 127
Online Resources · 5, 237
opportunity cost · 171, 178, 179, 195, 230
Option Pricing · 5, 215
Organization · 4, 130
overbidding · 138, 161, 164

P

Pedro Martinez · 110, 123, 142
perfect information · 22, 23
Piling On · 4, 142
Pitcher Abuse Points · 96
Pitcher Characteristics · 4, 94
Player Movement · 5, 180
Player Rater · 48, 50, 214
Player Unpredictability · 4, 104
player values · 9, 16, 52, 65, 76
point distribution ranges · 57
popularity · 9
position over value · 188, 189, 193, 208, 230
Position Planning · 5, 172
Position Scarcity · 4, 146
positional advantage · 114, 149
Predictability · 4, 145, 229
Price Adjustments · 4, 137
Price Inflation and Deflation · 5, 161
projections · 10, 16, 38, 47, 48, 50, 51, 52, 54, 55, 79, 128, 140, 157, 162, 163, 164
punt a category · 56

R

Randy Johnson · 73, 85, 109, 110, 142, 153
ranking systems · 50
Reading the Indicators · 3, 17
real estate tycoons · 22, 23
replacement player · 54, 57, 59, 66, 75, 89, 90, 108, 195
Roster Composition · 4, 154
roster constraints · 171
roster size · 170, 230
Rotisserie · 10, 13, 17
Roy Halladay · 94, 109, 110, 111

rules · 10, 13, 16, 39, 41, 52, 120, 127, 168, 171, 210, 211, 218
Rumors · 17, 181

S

salary cap · 69
scarcity · 148, 149, 150, 151, 229
self-interest · 36, 42, 84, 227
Soriano · 31, 32, 113, 129, 194, 211
Specialists · 4, 101, 103
speculate · 40, 50, 75, 169, 170, 179
spending · 6, 66, 78, 84, 91, 152, 163, 179, 180, 229, 235
Sportsline.com · 8
starter-optimized · 132
Starting Pitcher Injuries · 92
Starting pitchers · 89
straight draft · 126, 127
Strategies · 3, 11
Strategy Aids and Resources · 237
Strategy Checklist · 227
superior starter · 6, 88, 89, 90

T

Take It to Them · 3, 43
tally · 162
Tenacious Management Phenomenon · 3, 26, 34, 154
The Apathetic · 5, 205
The Cold Caller · 5, 200
The Draft is Only Half the Battle · 73
The Fundamental Theorem of Poker · 28
The Negotiator · 5, 201
The Persuader · 5, 203, 204
The Romantic · 5, 197
The Unpredictable · 5, 206
time value · 215, 218
trading · 184
trends · 24, 25, 34, 53, 54, 55, 152
Types of Trading Partners · 5, 197

U

Under Appreciated · 78
underbidding · 161, 164
Uneven player trades · 190
unexpectedly high level · 176
Unique Statistical Characteristics · 109
urgency close · 201
USA Today · 49, 51, 237

V

Valuation Example · 3, 54
Valuation Methodology · 3, 53
Valuation services · 61, 70
value creation · 43
value per dollar · 82
Vladimir Guerrero · 73, 113, 123, 130

W

When to find values · 72
Where to Find Bargains · 4, 71
Win, But Not By Too Much · 5, 184
winning this year · 154, 210
worksheet · 14
Worksheet for Strategy Development · 232

QUICK ORDER FORM

Website Orders: www.fantasybaseballstrategy.com

E-mail Orders: book@fantasybaseballstrategy.com

Postal Orders: Henry Lee
Squeaky Press
P.O. Box 4452
Mountain View, CA 94040-0452

Please send me ____ copies of the Fantasy Baseball Strategy Book. Enclosed is a check or money order for $24.95 per book plus shipping and any applicable tax. Check website for updated prices.

U.S. Shipping is $3.95 for the first book and $2.00 for each additional book. California residents please add 8.5% tax.

My total order amount is $_____

Send my book/s to:

Name:_____
Address:_____
_____
City/State/Zip:_____
Telephone:_____
E-mail Address:_____
Comments:_____

Printed in the United States
16200LVS00001B/26-38